Office Politics

Office Politics
Seizing Power
Wielding Clout

Marilyn Moats Kennedy

Follett Publishing Company
Chicago

Design by Karen Yops

Library of Congress Cataloging in Publication Data
Kennedy, Marilyn Moats, 1943–
  Office politics.
  1. Success. 2. Organizational behavior. 3. Industrial sociology. I. Title.
HF5386.K278   650′.14   79-23735
ISBN 0-695-81306-4

First Printing

DEDICATION

For my parents,
Orin and Georgia Moats,
who provided
the opportunity
for me to study journalism,
and for my husband,
Daniel Joseph Kennedy, Jr.,
who insisted I make
something of it

Contents

Acknowledgements

First, I wish to thank Deborah Lynn Panter, who left a very good job to work as my editorial assistant on this book. Without her patience, good judgment, encouragement, help in the research and editing, and occasional dog-walking, this book would still be aborning.

Second, let me thank Elaine Goldberg, managing editor at Follett Publishing Company, who encouraged me to write the book. I really had no intention of doing anything but talking about it, but she egged me on.

Third, let me thank the faculty of the Medill School of Journalism, Northwestern University, for the invaluable training I received there. I am especially grateful to Ben Baldwin, an exceptional teacher and critic.

Most of the research described in the book came about as a result of the need to help clients of Career Strategies, the career-planning and consulting firm I began in June 1975. My clients— almost ten thousand in all—have contributed substantially through their experiences and feedback. They have given hundreds of interviews and shared their experiences with me freely, for which I am deeply grateful. There are no personal experiences in the book simply because, compared with the problems some of my clients have faced, my own fade. I have tried in each case to use only experiences shared by a number of people—not the one, most outrageous case.

Most of the research was done during and after seminars between January 1977 and June 1979. The first seminar on office politics was done with Lynda Duncan Carney for DePaul University in 1977, and feedback from it provided the basic idea as well as much of the basic direction for this book.

The chapter on nonprofit organizations (chapter 9) is the result of many, many interviews with people who have worked, and currently are working, with such organizations. Most of these people demanded anonymity for reasons you will understand when you read that chapter.

The names and kinds of businesses but not their size or type (i.e., profit or nonprofit organization) have been changed in every case. We have disguised the individual who gave us the information completely, but we have kept the political characteristics of the organization intact. All cases have a factual base.

The research, ideas, and expressions of opinion are entirely my own, as is every word in the book. I stand accountable for what I've written.

Preface

This book is dedicated to the proposition that we all have choices. We can choose the skills we use on our job, the kind of job we take, and for whom and with whom we work. That's career planning. We can also use tools of analysis to look closely at the work environment before we begin a job—and then we can constantly make use of these tools on the job. That's practical politics as exercised in the office. Either we learn to manage the politics of our place of work, or we are its victims. It's as stark as that. You can learn how the process works, or you can fail. The choice is yours.

But most people don't believe this. They insist on the mythology of St. Horatio Alger. Even though his books have never been turned into a television miniseries, and if you read them today, they seem quaint and out of touch, he is still believed religiously. What Alger said was that if you worked really hard, pleased your boss, didn't make waves, and were ethical and morally upright, you'd rise to the top in business just like cream in a milk bottle.

While Alger was no Mark Twain (and is never even mentioned in college literature courses), there was no question that he was persuasive. All of Alger's heroes were boys who began life

11

in poor circumstances and rose to success through hard work. I read and understood the message and believed it.

I believed in the work ethic fervently. If I worked hard, and if I were very competent, I would succeed. I did not meet Niccolò Machiavelli until I was a student at Northwestern University.

Machiavelli said flat out that the political process was a vital part of human organizations, and that you couldn't get away from it. The political process controlled who got what, when, and how. It was a short leap from world or local governmental politics to the politics of the work place.

I soon found out. I graduated and went to work. Like most of the people who will read this book, I resisted the idea that office politics was a fact of every person's working life. I believed that if, as Alger said, I worked very hard and behaved ethically, I'd beat the system. I haven't. What I have discovered, which I share with my readers, is how to make office politics work for, rather than against, a person's career.

Until you understand why the myths we live by are false, you'll always be a victim. As long as you believe that, out there somewhere, there's a universal definition of hard work that you can know and meet, you will be unpleasantly surprised at every contact point with the world of work. You will be seriously disappointed as you discover that nobody understands, much less shares, your idea of what constitutes hard work.

As long as you believe that performance appraisal can be valuefree, and that your employer can and will lay aside his or her personal values and prejudices to look at your work objectively, you are going to be miserable.

As long as you believe that people, including yourself perhaps, are fired because they are incompetent and can't do the job, you'll never understand how you or anybody else comes to be abruptly unemployed.

As long as you believe that all actions in the office are based on fairness and rationality, you'll be hurt, confused, and disillusioned.

Finally, as long as you look for a formula for success, you are doomed to frustration. There are as many formulas as there are work environments and bosses managing them. You don't have to make the same mistakes over and over—or even once. Read on.

Office Politics

Chapter 1

Working Myths—*or* Why Horatio Alger Was Wrong

Once upon a time two young people, Harry and Elizabeth, stood poised on the college steps ready to enter the working world full-time. Both had had part-time jobs. Both had shiny new degrees that reflected some job skills. Both were attuned to the myths and values that permeated American society. Neither was more than ordinarily naive.

Harry and Elizabeth expected to work hard. They were both so delighted to have jobs that they had little thought of changing the business world. The goal of each was to adjust to the work environment and make a success of the first job. While Harry might occasionally speak cynically about business, or Elizabeth might talk of the "pigs" one could expect to meet in executive suites, both were imbued with an honest belief that they understood the rules of business and, given a reasonable chance, would make a success of their careers.

Because they were intelligent young people, Harry and Elizabeth had each chosen a first job with great care. They had, on the advice of the college placement office, asked perceptive questions in the fashion of the day; looked around at the work environment; screened the boss carefully within their limited frame of knowledge; and, in the end, plunged—trusting to the Almighty and luck that the choice would work out.

15

Within six months both Harry and Elizabeth were looking for new jobs. Harry had been fired for insubordination. This had consisted of suggesting that a particular task might be done differently from the way in which it had always been done. When Harry raised this point a second time, he was told that things "aren't working out around here." Since he was on three months' probation as a new employee, he was terminated for cause.

Elizabeth was still employed at that time but frantically typing résumés and going on lunch-hour interviews. Her boss kept hinting that at the first performance appraisal—three months in the future—she could expect a negative rating. Elizabeth felt that she was the victim of some kind of plot to get rid of her. She worked hard, got on well with her co-workers, and really did what she was supposed to do. Why didn't the boss like her?

One night Harry and Elizabeth ran into each other in a singles' bar. They were both shell-shocked and began comparing war stories. As they talked, it occurred to them that somehow a part of their education had been neglected or was missing. Both sets of parents had explained that there was probably a lot of politics (whatever that was) in most offices. Still, office politics is not something the average college student has had enough experience with to be able to call by name when confronted with it.

After a few drinks, Harry and Elizabeth agreed to meet in a few weeks for mutual support. Each moved on to a new job shortly—definitely sadder but not particularly wiser.

Harry and Elizabeth's experience is duplicated by millions of young—and not so young—people every day. The best kept secret in a transparent society is that office politics exists and affects every working person's career. If we are not to spend our working lives repeating Harry and Elizabeth's experience in our own careers, we're going to have to bring office politics out of the closet. There's no way to deal with it unless we acknowledge its existence, examine the process, and act on what we learn.

Office politics is to the office what power politics is to any level of government—a process for getting things done. It contains many of the same elements and maneuvers. Executives compete for power, responsibility, resources, and money. Secretaries jockey for position, using intricate methods of backstabbing and backbiting. Managers struggle to curry favor higher up while placating the troops below. And everyone barters for favors with a great deal of relish, push, and shove.

These processes are integral to office politics, and office politics is an integral part of every organization, whether it be profit or nonprofit, in the public or private sector, large or small, sophisticated or simple. There is no such thing as a politically sterile environment. There never can be when two or more people work together.

While there are similarities between real politics and office politics, there are also important differences. Most of the people who define themselves as politicians have chosen politics as a career and a life-style. These people talk among themselves about the fact that they are engaged in the pursuit of power, allegedly for the public good. They act in the name of the public and use whatever means are needed to reach their ends, sometimes legitimate and sometimes not. They reserve their facades and hypocrisy for publication and outsiders only, while discussing tactics and strategies among themselves.

Most people in offices, shops, and factories, however, have not chosen politics as a way of life nor ever thought of it as a tool for getting things done. If they are aware of the political process at all, they think of it as a giant negative in their working lives. Seizing power and wielding clout are not their top priorities. They see themselves as trying to reduce the level of involvement in the process. They may even say that they chose their work because they didn't want the push and shove of government politics. "Politics is a dirty business," they say.

Another difference between politics in government and in the office is that people in the office isolate themselves from reality. They cannot or will not acknowledge the fact that politics plays an important part in getting things done. They don't like to admit that we are all politicians, whatever we're called.

All of us are limited by our own myths and perceptions of what is going on. If people are aware of the political process at all, it's not something they talk about openly. The general philosophy is, "If we ignore it, it doesn't exist." That attitude compounds political problems. Hardly anyone with more than a few years' work experience has not seen or personally experienced the pain involved in losing a political battle in the office, or in being sidetracked or sideswiped.

The younger the person, the greater the sense of bewilderment and the more Kafkaesque the flavor office politics seems to have. The differences between what people expect and what they find often leave beginning workers depressed. This depression is not limited to the young. In fact, many experienced people charge everything they can't explain and every career setback to office politics. They have seen enough victims of the process to be able to identify people about to fail. Still, they cannot rationally explain how the other person got into that spot. That is why, when someone is fired in an office, and nobody can really see what the person has done—or failed to do—to earn so harsh a penalty, the victim is chalked up to office politics. Unable to identify what part of the political process resulted in the downfall, onlookers fault the whole process. Many people feel that the best way to cope is to ignore the whole thing—as if noninvolvement were possible or could change things.

Office politics is bewildering for most people because what we experience is clearly at odds with what we believe. We believe that hard work leads to success. Society encourages us to believe this. After all, if working hard doesn't equal success, what does? The problem is that most of us know people who live out the myth—working very hard, doing a good job, not annoying anyone higher up, and working amiably with their peers—but who never get ahead. They may even be fired. Clearly something else is involved in the success equation besides hard work and amiability. We see a clearly indifferent performer who doesn't work particularly hard climb the ladder with apparent ease. Still we cling to the myth of hard work, though, at gut level, we know something else must be a part of the question.

But what is it? We keep looking for easy answers. Look at the popularity of "how-to-succeed" books and courses, motivational theory, organizational theory, and theory theory. We are desperately searching for some clue to explain why reality is so very different from the myth. What are the answers? Why don't the people with the most experience give these answers to those with the least experience?

Probably the least attractive part of the hard-work myth is that it encourages hypocrisy on the part of people who know that office politics has a great deal to do with who gets what, when, and how. When people who have made it continue to mouth platitudes about working hard, not making enemies, being ambitious, and so on, instead of explaining the political facts of life to the young, it encourages a quasi-Victorian conspiracy of silence.

The Victorians clung to the hope that if they did not talk about sex, it would go away. They could not bring themselves to talk publicly about the fact that sex was vitally important, an indispensable part of life, and even potentially interesting and fun. The same is true of office politics. Giving office politics the silent treatment or undervaluing its critical importance will never improve anyone's ability to get along in the working world. This conspiracy of silence is not limited to any one kind of worker. Masters of Business Administration programs talk about the theory of power structures and hierarchies but rarely mention practical politics in the office. They seem to avoid the issue. Instead, they present a theoretical business world that is competitive but never vicious, one in which political factors play little part. People make decisions on hardheaded, profit-and-loss bases—not on emotional hot flashes.

This conspiracy of silence has left the novice worker frustrated and the veteran numb and cynical. Any change in either's ability to cope or change attitudes has to begin with an analysis and rethinking of the five work myths that condition our working lives and control our responses to office politics. (We will examine these myths later on in this chapter.) Otherwise, office politics will continue to be random, terrifying, and inexplicable. People's careers will seem to be a matter of good luck or bad, of friends or enemies, of success or victimization, or of the old story of the star's having been "in the right place at the right time."

WHY EXAMINE THE MYTHS?

It's time to take office politics out of the closet and examine the process openly. Without careful analysis there can be no choice; all the choices you make will be prompted either by whim or by desperation. There are four reasons for learning how to analyze the internal politics of your organization or of any organization you might propose to join.

First, once you examine the political climate of your organization, you'll have the information needed to make informed career choices. You'll know whether management sees you as retainable or promotable. You'll know which elements of the work environment cause you the most difficulty and what things to avoid when you change jobs.

Second, you will have the know-how to work within the political process to do the things you need and want to do. If you want to increase your visibility with management, you will be able to do so. If you want to move ahead, you'll be able to develop a plan to do this.

Third, you'll be able to exert greater control as a supervisor or manager over your own employees. You can help reduce conflict within your own working unit and increase both productivity and job satisfaction.

Finally, you can improve your own job satisfaction by reducing unnecessary anxiety and political conflict, thereby raising your own productivity. No expert, real or self-proclaimed, would champion the idea that terrorized employees are more productive than reasonably secure ones in the long run. Terrorized employees will either leave or eventually sabotage their own positions through deliberate or careless mistakes.

Any attempt to reduce the level of political discomfort begins by examining the five working myths that dominate our working lives. We're going to look at each one independently and then relate these myths to the work environment overall.

The five myths to which most of us subscribe are:

1. Hard work equals success. If you work diligently you will get ahead.

2. People who get fired from their jobs are incompetent. They simply don't know enough or aren't skilled or experienced enough to do the job.

3. Performance appraisal is a fair assessment of what you can do and what you have done in the past.

4. Office politics is a nasty game of bad people doing evil things to good people—much like warfare.

5. You either understand innately how office politics works or you don't. Some people are naturally savvy. The rest can't learn.

THE MYTH OF HARD WORK

Most of us cling fiercely to the belief that if we work hard and are competent, we will get ahead. This ignores the important fact that hard work has no universally agreed upon definition or standard of measurement such as an inch, yard, or mile. Hard work is certainly never specified in quantitative terms. Do people who work hard sweat more than people who don't? Maybe, but not necessarily. Does hard work mean producing more of whatever the product is? It may, but it does not always relate quality to output. Does hard work include the way in which one works—style as opposed to productivity? Are cheerful, outgoing people harder workers than less pleasant types?

The fact is that hard work is situational. The person with the most power defines hard work in every work situation. Hard work depends on what your boss—and generally his or her boss—says it is. This is true whether productivity is fairly easy to measure, typing for instance, or more difficult, as is the case for many management jobs.

This would be easy to follow if the boss or boss's boss explained his or her definitions and operating assumptions. All employees who reported to either of them could decide whether they would do whatever the boss wanted in the way he or she wanted it done. The choice would be clear. Unfortunately, most bosses do not define hard work or explain how they plan to measure what the employee does.

The boss may not even be aware that what he or she says is at variance with what he or she really wants and expects. The boss may not even be aware that he or she is mixing work content with style.

This means that the hard-work equation is not hard work equals success but hard work equals style plus results, both of which are defined by the boss. As a result, production is often overshadowed by style, that is, the way in which the person does his or her work. Therefore, people who say "I work hard and nobody appreciates me, recognizes this, or rewards me" are confused. Whose definition of hard work is being used? Is it the individual's? Where did that definition come from? Does anyone agree with it? The most common political problems people have arise from a misunderstanding of what a particular boss means by hard work. If a worker develops his or her own independent standard, it will almost always fail to take account of the boss's standard.

There . y to define hard work outside the context of the

specific work environment defined and managed by a specific boss. Misunderstandings most often occur because people believe they are hired to do jobs "to the best of their abilities" or "as they see fit." They don't understand that they are going to be judged on the methods (work style) they use as well as on the results. If they never correctly perceive what the job is, then no matter how much work they do, it will never be enough because it won't be the right kind of work in the right style.

You can test this statement very easily by recalling times when your work changed entirely when the boss left and a new boss took control. Not only did the actual tasks you did change, but also the way you talked about your work and your relationship with those around you. Bosses create the political environment and reshape it in response to the dynamics of the organization and to their own needs and levels of comfort.

For example, let's consider Leslie's problem. After five years with Greater Dynamic Book Purveyors, Leslie was named supervisor of the word-processing group. Fifteen part-time and thirty full-time people reported to her, both men and women. At the time Leslie accepted the promotion, her boss told her how important productivity was. "This unit has got to put out more words per worker every day if we're to do the job right," she said. Having gotten what she saw as a clear mandate, Leslie began to push her people to produce roughly 20 percent more than had been the standard in the past.

In three months the frost in the word-processing department was visible. Turnover was rising; Leslie's stomach and nervous system were deteriorating. Her boss called her into her office and said that she didn't think Leslie was doing the job as well as the boss had thought she could. When Leslie reminded her boss of their original conversation and the boss's concern with productivity, the boss said, "Look, I said productivity was most important, but you've got to use common sense. Getting people all upset over an artificially high standard isn't good supervision." Leslie began looking for another job—convinced that her boss was unreasonable and irrational.

Another example is Jeff, a production worker. Jeff has had fewer quality-control problems than anyone else in his section. Unfortunately, he has a personality that will strip paint from woodwork at ten feet. His effect on other workers is to depress their production. Jeff argues that he works very hard, produces quality work, and should be evaluated solely on his production. Jeff's boss does not see it that way. He will continue to hold Jeff back because of his abrasive personality. To the boss, good peer relationships are as important as, or more important than, absolute productivity.

The major point, of course, is that the myth of hard work is not an absolute but an abstract. In not recognizing this, people often are confronted by the second job myth: job failure.

THE MYTH OF JOB FAILURE

Job failure means being fired from a job, being asked to resign, or leaving a job voluntarily because you had very strong evidence that one of these two was your impending fate. Managers and workers alike subscribe wholeheartedly to the myth that people are fired because they're incompetent. This incompetence may take any form from personality problems to skills problems. Since anyone who has worked anywhere for more than a month can pick out the workers he or she personally sees as incompetent, the myth seems to reflect reality. The complication is that the people workers identify as incompetent don't always get fired—even though they cost the organization thousands of dollars as well as their fellow workers' untold time and aggravation, and even though such people have bad attitudes to boot. Many retire after long service with full corporate honors.

You can't expect to understand why people get fired or are forced to leave until you look at the myth of job failure. In order to understand that, we have to review how people are hired into an organization.

If you look at the typical hiring process, you will be struck by the fact that, despite the personnel department's efforts to screen all applicants with care, a certain percentage of failures sneak through. Of all the people hired, a certain percentage will be fired, be asked to leave, or will leave because they anticipate being fired or asked to leave. This is true regardless of (1) the amount of screening that precedes the hiring, (2) the work to be done on the job, (3) the level of skill needed to do the work, and (4) the skill or lack of skill of the managers for whom these people work. Two reasons explain these hiring failures: either the persons were misjudged on their ability to do the job, or they lacked the skills in office politics to work within that specific work environment.

Political failures are never identified as such on termination reports and only rarely in exit interviews. Instead, one reads of "inability to get along well with others," "disruptive personality," "failure to establish good working relationships with peers," "too emotional," "unprofessional conduct," and so on. How do we know that these terms cover up a political problem? It may be that the person who was fired does have a "disruptive personality," but so do some of those who have remained

Look at what the people who have left or been fired say. They respond in the same vein. "The boss didn't like me," they say; "The boss played favorites and I wasn't one of them"; "People didn't like me and I didn't much like them"; "It was too political"; or "It wasn't my kind of company." The implication is that the boss was OK and the worker a real reject, an incompetent.

But something is amiss. Both employers and employees are talking about particular kinds of people problems (not personality problems) that are completely tied to one particular work environment.

In other words, a person with a personality problem as opposed to a work-environment problem should fail time after time because his or her personality is consistent over time. Others should respond to such employees fairly consistently, regardless of the type or size of the organization or the nature of the work. But that is not what happens. Instead, a man or woman who is fired from Bank A as someone with very poor people skills can go to work happily and productively for Bank B in the very same kind of job and be thought by peers and superiors to be "very good with people," "well liked," and "well respected." The people environment can make it possible or impossible for anyone, regardless of personality or level of skill, to do a job well. It is the boss who controls and sets the tone in the people environment.

The simple solution is to improve employee selection so that Bank A never hires the person in our example. This would eliminate job failures based on political rather than skill deficiencies. The problem is that even though personnel departments are aware that people fail in some environments and succeed in others, they lack the power to dissuade managers from conventional selection methods. Personnel departments have great incentive to develop better screening tools in order to protect their own interests, but they can rarely sell these tools to management.

Many techniques have been developed to measure job skills. Some of the most successful include typing and shorthand tests. A person either can or cannot type and take shorthand at a certain speed with a certain degree of accuracy. These skills are measurable, and the standards of what constitutes good performance can be set throughout an organization. Far less successful are efforts to measure such skills as organizational ability, planning, supervision, management, time management, and so on, though, like a cure for cancer, someone always promises that it can be done. Personnel journals discuss the selection process regularly, but so far the tools of analysis are as primitive as the stone ax.

Judging how any one worker will get along with and cooperate with other workers has been largely ignored. Where are the tools for assessing whether or not Applicant A will be able to work productively with Boss B? Since this is by far the most difficult screening problem, personnel people have been glad to leave it to "managerial prerogative." This term covers everything personnel or the manager wants left to subjective judgment.

In the never-ending battle to take the risk out of choosing employees, some companies have turned to "personality testing" or "psychological testing." Many of these tests concentrate on an overall picture of the applicant's personality and values. It's a pretty poor applicant who can't thwart the tests. Many refuse to take them at all. There is no evidence that those who refuse are less able or have more personality problems than those who agree. In fact, the noncooperators may be more confident of their ability to get another job. They would be less likely to put up with what rightly may be seen as an invasion of privacy. While the results of such tests may be somewhat interesting, this kind of overview gives little insight into the potential fit between employer and employee. It might be more interesting to give the boss the same test and match the scores. Still, the results would be open to question.

Requiring the boss to take the same test each time he or she wants to hire a new subordinate (because people may change over time) would be viewed as outrageous by both the personnel department and individual managers. It would also be impractical, expensive, and time-consuming. Besides, managers frequently ignore the results of personality or psychological tests in making a hiring decision. They feel that since they are going to live with the decision, they'd best use judgment instead of science or pseudoscience. The selection process gives no clue as to how any boss will get on with any applicant in a particular work environment. Nor does it determine priorities.

Is it more important that the secretary be able to type eighty words a minute with no errors, or that he or she be compatible with the boss and able to work effectively with other secretaries? How will either the boss or the secretary make a decision in the standard thirty- to sixty-minute employment interview? The personnel department's screening interview verified the facts of the new secretary's job history. That initial interview was not set up to screen him or her for potential compatibility with a particular boss. Both boss and worker take a large risk when they decide to work together. Both probably assume that it will work out if they are "both professionals" or try to get along together.

After a few weeks or months, if one or both realize that the working relationship has no future, neither will necessarily have learned anything from the experience. Folk wisdom says, "Bad fit," whatever that is. The secretary may say, "I can't work for nitpickers; they make me break out in a rash." The boss may say, "Next time send me somebody who really cares about precision and accuracy. Gloria Smith didn't have it. Oh, she typed fast enough, but she got nervous when I checked her work." The issue between them is a matter of personal style, not a matter of competence.

Who gets hired and how it works out is largely a result of trial and error. It may take both the boss and the secretary four, six, or even eight trials before each finds a person who is compatible and with whom each can work within the particular work environment.

Job failure is complicated by the fact that the secretary who quits, rather than waiting to be fired, will be categorized differently by the personnel department. It will not be called a termination. This tends to distort the truth. Yet in fact, this was a failure because the secretary couldn't work for and with the boss.

Job failure, in all cases, is an entirely subjective judgment. People can quit for a variety of reasons, ranging from getting a better job to fear of being fired. Job failure, as we mean it, is intended to cover only situations in which the person believed that the hot breath of termination was on his or her neck and so leapt out of the job before being pushed.

It's a real social stigma to fail. Few people will admit to family or close friends, let alone strangers, that they've been fired. People will give up severance pay rather than have it said aloud, much less recorded, that they were fired. There is no question that across the board, workers see being fired as a job failure that raises self-doubt and calls their competence into question.

The greatest fear of job hunters is that it will be known that they were fired and that they will never get another job as a result. If it were true that firing consigned people to the employment junkyard, the true unemployment rate would be about 50 percent! It's nowhere near that high, but job hunters ignore the facts and remain concerned about having been fired.

In the past two years we have interviewed more than a thousand persons who have had job failures in about thirty-five different kinds of jobs. In our research we talked not only to the person who had failed at the job but also to many of the bosses of those people. Neither knew the other would be interviewed. The surprising thing was that, in the majority of cases, both sides agreed that the problem that precipitated the failure was a political rather than a skills problem.

The results of these interviews showed that only 25 percent of the people failed because they couldn't do the job technically. Personnel departments, which work nonstop to keep out all but the most hopelessly overqualified applicants, can take credit for some of this. Seventy-five percent, the overwhelming majority, failed because they were unskilled in office politics in one of three ways. They were (1) unable to get along with the boss, (2) unable to get along with peers, or (3) unable to go along with organizational values. Some people had all three problems, but one generally overwhelmed the other two.

Thirty-five percent of the 75 percent group said that they failed because they could not get along with the boss. This most often meant incompatibility either of values or of work styles. Responses ranged from "The boss doesn't like me" to "I could never understand what he [she] wanted me to do." The boss, when interviewed, would say, "He [she] never got a handle on what I wanted done. He [she] required too much supervision."

The employee pointed out, "The boss never put forth a complete thought the whole time I was there. He [she] couldn't give directions, and when he [she] did, no one could follow them." A favorite refrain was, "I wasn't the only one."

Another common response from employees was "We had frequent conflicts over what needed to be done and what I should be doing." It would be an oversimplification to say that these were communications problems. Both sides were communicating, but through different value screens and at different levels, each choosing what to receive from the other. It's a mistake to assume that either side *couldn't* understand if by "couldn't" we mean a technical impossibility. It was more often a problem of each side hearing or understanding what he or she believed was said or meant. This is not a new problem and affects all kinds of relationships—personal as well as business.

Twenty-five percent of the people in the survey said that they could not get along with, or win acceptance from, their peers and subordinates. This was true even when everyone recognized that cooperation was critical to getting the job done. It's a fact in most organizations that work is cooperative rather than strongly competitive. Few people complete a project from start to finish without help from others. Most are involved in a process of receiving work from one source, processing that work, and passing it on. If a person is disliked enough by his or her peers, these people will find ways to set up the person for failure.

Employees who are doing the fifth-column work may or may not be motivated by their own career needs. The effect is the same. The person going through the job failure has failed to sell his or her peers on cooperation rather than sabotage. Peers can sabotage this person by losing or forgetting the information needed to do a particular job, by giving the grapevine enough half-truths to cause subordinates to doubt the person's ability or mandate to lead, or by seeing that a person is tagged with responsibility for a collective failure. If that person's political failure has included failure to please his or her own boss, the boss can ratify or contribute to this scapegoating procedure.

For instance, Jack had been brought into a department as heir apparent to the current manager. At least two men and one woman had believed themselves in line for the manager's job. Although the manager who designated Jack as the heir should have been the target of their collective wrath, they turned on Jack instead. The strategy was to make him look like a boob and thus reopen the question of succession. Jack found himself the object of guerrilla warfare, including a whispering campaign fueled by mistakes he'd made in a similar job four years before (which shouldn't even have been known in the new organization), a deliberate exclusion from all informal meetings, and the denial of even a "hello" from the triumvirate. His interoffice mail was delayed for three or four days so that he got notices only hours or minutes before meetings were to start. This made him seem unprepared. When he complained to his boss about the mail, his complaint was dismissed as paranoia. The boss never believed that the triumvirate would behave in such an aggressive manner.

After one month, the triumvirate goaded Jack into fighting back. He began telling people at random what was going on. This displeased his boss, who thought Jack should have "toughed it out." In four months the boss was talking about *whether* Jack should succeed him rather than *when.* Jack left.

The final 15 percent in our survey left or were fired because they could not accept the values of the organization, as they understood or saw them acted out by their supervisors. If the organization valued a particularly aggressive behavior, these employees refused to go along. If the organization rewarded a certain group spirit, they were recluses and shunned their co-workers.

A common example of this group is people who've gone to work for cigarette companies or oil companies only to decide that their personal values are not the same as those of their organization. If they aren't fired for some work-related failure, they tend to become involved in sabotage, and thus force management to fire them.

Among people between the ages of twenty-five and thirty-five, company loyalty was a major stumbling block. Many bosses expected loyalty, and these people were unable to give it. They had a tendency to reject organizations in which employees talked about how good the company was to its employees as well as other employees who showed any booster spirit. In fact, one of the outstanding characteristics of Vietnam-era workers— those who reached twenty-one between 1968 and 1972—is their utter lack of institutional loyalty. These people can't relate to the organization as an organization. They have a very low tolerance level for anyone who mentions "company loyalty." The most loyalty many of them can manage is loyalty to an immediate boss. As a result, these people tend to focus on a particular boss when they hunt for a job. The overall organization doesn't exist for them except to serve as a cradle that holds the boss, the job, and themselves.

This means that management's selling the company qua company in an interview was no sell at all. These workers drew no reflected glory from working for the "biggest," the "best," the "oldest," or the "most prestigious" organization. The effect on nonprofit organizations was especially devastating, as many of these organizations had paid their employees off for years in prestige rather than in money. Our interviews turned up many agency heads who saw the lack of worker loyalty as a major problem in recruiting and retaining staff.

All the people who had political failures shared one important insight into their own failure. They saw themselves out of sync with the others in their work environment. They talked about the isolation that signaled their political failure and impending doom. Isolating the person who is failing appears to be a common thread that ties together both skill failures and political failures. It's almost as if other workers think that being fired, like VD, may be catching.

The actual firing ranged from unpleasant to brutal. Because of the social stigma attached to firing, the employee was always shocked, if not surprised. A political firing was far more likely to damage the worker's self-image and ego than was a skills firing because the worker could not be sure that the reason given was the real reason. As a result, the employee took such a firing very personally.

Firing employees will continue to be a fact of organizational life. It will continue to be painful to both sides. But if the firing is apt to have political roots, an examination of office politics can help diagnose potential explosions while they are still in the shudder stage. People can bail out of hopeless situations with some choices and retain some dignity.

THE MYTH OF PERFORMANCE APPRAISAL

Next to low-calorie gin, there is nothing employees would like better than fair, reasoned performance reviews. They want to know how the productivity standard is set, what it is, how productive they've been, and, finally, whether they have the potential to advance.

Every work-appraisal system—whether it's called a performance appraisal, work assessment, performance review, feedback, evaluation, or progress report—is supposed to give both manager and worker a definite fix on how well the worker does his or her job. The system may or may not be tied to a salary review. Some experts contend that discussion of money limits the exchange of ideas. In most organizations, the system is based on the assumption that there are certain performance standards that apply to all employees across the board, and that these standards ensure fairness.

Getting to work on time is an example. There are also job-tied standards that should help evaluation vis-à-vis one particular job. The system assumes a godlike impartiality on the part of the evaluator. The evaluator is assumed to be capable of a fair, balanced, well thought out evaluation of the employee's work, free of prejudices and personal feelings.

That constitutes the theory. In fact, whatever the real merits of performance-appraisal systems—the born-again cynics call them personality- or political-skills appraisal systems—they are almost universally eyed with suspicion and trepidation by perpetrators and victims alike.

Managers acknowledge that personality plays a large part in performance appraisal. They realize that they like some employees better than others. There are clashes in values and work styles that have nothing to do with productivity. Even personnel departments aren't totally sold on the concept of review—especially after they've talked with some of the victims of bizarre applications. As the personnel director of a large company said, "Look, there is no way to keep a manager from using the performance-appraisal system to club a subordinate he or she either doesn't want to promote or actively wants to get rid of. I've seen performance appraisal used as part of guerrilla warfare against people a manager couldn't fire but wanted to. All personnel can do is pick up the pieces."

Even experts in the field can find much to criticize in both theory and practice. Kenneth F. Herrold in *The Handbook of Modern Personnel Administration* acknowledges some of these problems when he points out that people who favor performance appraisal rarely agree among themselves on guidelines or methods or even on how to evaluate the results.* He further suggests that the results are rarely reliable or useful, and that the programs as enacted seem to be "haphazard, inconsistent, ritualistic," and sometimes may "violate human rights."

What's even more interesting is that it made little difference to people whether their appraisal was good or bad, fair or not. If their performance appraisal was reasonable, they could still cite people under the same system who had been treated unreasonably. If their appraisal wasn't fair, they were the victims. Those who advanced were equally as unhappy with the system as those who did not. This probably stemmed from the fact that, knowing that even if they had slipped through the system this year, the whole dreary, unfair, value-laden process would have to be gone through again in six or twelve months.

Workers went so far as to question the idea that there was anything systematic about performance-appraisal systems. As one construction superintendent said, "What system? System means there's a theory of how something works and whether it will work a certain way most of the time. You sure couldn't say that about any performance-appraisal system I've ever seen!" Personnel experts tend to agree that the greatest weakness of even the most carefully designed system is its inability to work as a system. Top management has difficulty keeping itself or middle management from implementing the guidelines as each sees fit—however arbitrary that may be.

In researching individual reactions to performance appraisals, certain themes stood out. There was almost universal agreement on the following:

1. Performance appraisal theory never matches the practice. People see performance appraisal as a mask for the boss's

*Kenneth F. Herrold, "Principles and Techniques of Assessment," in Joseph F. Famularo, ed., *Handbook of Modern Personnel Administration* (New York: McGraw-Hill Book Company, 1972), pp. 40–43.

hidden agenda. If the boss doesn't like Lucy's personality and style, it will be reflected in her appraisal. Regardless of productivity, the boss will remark negatively on Lucy's style. This apparent unfairness is built into the system because any evaluation will be through somebody's screen of values. There is no such thing as a value-free evaluation. Lucy may or may not be aware of what is going on, but she will see herself as unfairly treated if productivity is supposed to be the measure when, in fact, it's her personality.

Bosses themselves are not above mouthing the platitude that "it's performance that counts." The most famous rebuttal to that is Lee Iacocca, now chairman of the board of Chrysler Corporation and former president of Ford Motor Company. When Iacocca was fired by Henry Ford in the summer of 1978, there was no question that Iacocca was fired for violating his boss's hidden agenda and values rather than for any kind of nonperformance or ineptness. Iacocca was the father of the Ford Mustang, one of Ford's most successful cars. Still, the car is named the Ford Mustang, not the Iacocca Mustang.

A number of press accounts of the firing talked of Iacocca's "pressing Ford too hard." In no published account attributed to a person or to "informed sources" did Henry Ford, any of his aides, or anyone else in Detroit suggest that Iacocca's performance was substandard. That he was judged by criteria other than performance results seems indisputable.

2. Performance appraisal has little to do with money. People criticize performance-appraisal systems because they are rarely tied to the money-reward system. Many nonprofit organizations are in the habit of telling employees, "Your performance this year has been great, but we have no money and therefore can't give you a raise—or even a cost-of-living increase." Another nonprofit favorite is to give the same percentage across the board, regardless of merit. David, who works for the world's wealthiest organization, rarely sees this as charitable and indicts himself for failing. He thinks that had he really understood the system, he would have gotten a raise. If the organization truly valued him, it would have come up with the money or a promotion. This self-indictment is largely justified. Both nonprofit and profit organizations do find money for employees they want to retain, however arbitrary the method of selection. The absolute emphasis on money stems from the very American attitude that if money doesn't change hands, it's not real work and not valued. Look at the attitudes toward people who do volunteer work and women working at home, housewives!

In some organizations there are official rules setting forth the relationship between money and performance. A bank in Atlanta has been known to fire employees who ask for raises. Money is a taboo. Why does management think people are working for the bank? Money is never to be brought up by employees. Management (at the very top) will make such allocations as seem reasonable. The result is to reduce the importance of performance and increase the importance of political games. "Can I make my boss mention money? How much?"

By entirely separating raises and promotions from performance appraisal, the employee must really campaign for the dollar rather than perform and have that performance rewarded. Michael will spend more time worrying about pleasing his boss than doing his job. The effect is to take his mind off the job and put it on finding the hot buttons that will produce the dollars.

3. Performance appraisal uses measurements that are too abstract to measure anything. The criteria used and applied in performance-appraisal systems may be so vague that the appraisal is no more than the boss's opinion versus the employee's opinion. A favorite in the late 1970s has been the rating of performance on a scale of one to five—surely the last absurdity the already disreputable system can offer. For example:

1	2	3	4	5
OUTSTANDING	VERY GOOD	GOOD	NEEDS IMPROVEMENT	UNSATISFACTORY

If this bears a suspicious likeness to the old elementary- and secondary-school grading scale—which any schoolchild will tell you carries a built-in teacher bias—it may be that the people who develop these systems have run out of ideas. There might be some justification for the one to five or A to F scale in school when the evaluation period is shorter. To cover a full year's work and sum it up on a scale of from one to five does not strike the average, thinking worker as precise, fair, or reliable.

4. People skills are more important to good evaluations than productivity. Performance-appraisal systems tend to favor the articulate person, the assertive person, the person with good people skills. Those people who work very hard but very quietly will tend to be undervalued by their superiors, unless the superiors are like-minded, because they are easy to overlook. Instead of rewarding the quiet people, the tendency is to offer a promotion or a raise to Joe, who asks for it and who may leave if he doesn't get it. Nobody would necessarily miss Joe, but the idea of his departure would bother management. This way of distributing rewards mocks the system and confirms that performance appraisal doesn't measure performance or reward those who get the job done. (These people are sometimes called "donkeys." The implication is that they are needed to get the job done but faceless and going nowhere. If they were upwardly mobile, why would they be called donkeys?)

We could go on and on with this dreary litany, recounting all kinds of awful things that are done to reasonably competent men and women in the name of performance appraisal, but that would obscure the most important point. In the end, it doesn't really matter why people don't believe in the performance appraisal system as misapplied to them. What matters is what they do to counteract the system and to advance their own interests. What they do is get involved with office politics and learn the rules of the process. They call it "playing" politics.

THE MYTH OF OFFICE WARFARE

This leads to the fourth myth: Office politics is a nasty game during which bad people do evil things to innocent, decent people. This is really a composite of people's views on those they see around them who have good people skills and good political skills. It's more of a gut reaction than a reasoned response. This is false, of course, because almost everybody gets involved in politics periodically and, as we'll learn, politics is no game. It's worth our time to examine this view because people who feel this way are in the majority, probably 70-80 percent of the working population.

When you analyze this myth, you see two things immediately. First, most people see themselves as victims. They see no way of controlling events. They are perpetually done in and done to. Second, the majority of people see office politics as a war game between good and evil.

By casting every discussion of office politics as a moral issue, people absolve themselves of any need to participate. They create a lot of their own victimization. Nonparticipation, as we have discussed, simply is not an option. If we want nonparticipation, however, it's much easier to justify it when we wear white hats and the opposition wears black hats. Everyone must be either entirely good or entirely bad.

Office politics is a process. Anyone can use any part of the process to hurt or help anyone else. That it's occasionally used for evil purposes has no effect on the value of the process, or on the workings of the process.

As long as the myth persists that in office politics "good" people are always the victims of "evil" people, it will be impossible to rationally examine the process. This also keeps people who might be tempted to challenge an adverse performance rating from doing so. "What's the use?" they say. "The system is against me. I'm just one person, and my boss won't change anything anyway."

Most damaging to the average person's participation in the politics of his or her workplace is the emphasis on games. "Office politics is a game," people say. That word implies winning and losing, strategies without a real stake in the outcome, and a competitive, rather than cooperative, venture. The result is to discourage people who don't want to play games but do hope to get along. As long as the myth persists that we're playing games, those who see themselves as ill-equipped for gamesmanship will try to limit their own participation, even if it limits their careers.

The games people play in the office tend to be of two kinds. First, people try to find out who affects their careers and then impress those persons. Second, they try to undercut their peers and competitors. Since they don't have any system for doing either of these, it may be very haphazard and sometimes crude and brutal. If they can't impress the boss and build a working rapport, they will tend to backpedal for a while and then move out of the department. More often they will move out of the organization.

This leads to the final myth that dominates our working lives. In many ways it's the most pernicious of all.

THE MYTH OF POLITICAL SAVVY

You either understand office politics or you don't. Some people are political animals, the rest can't learn. You can imagine where most people put themselves. We hear a nonstop acceptance of the idea that nobody can learn about office politics. You're born a political animal or learn in the cradle, and that's it. All systems are put in place, and you have to wait twenty years to be able to use what came to you as a birthright.

This is absurd. Everything is learned, and no child has an innate sense of power politics at age six months. Because office politics is seen as both a game and an innate talent, people's behavior in the office tends to reflect the dichotomy. Unfortunately, no one told them the rules of the workplace before they were in the thick of battle.

It usually takes from three weeks to six months to learn the new job. It may take less time or as much as eight months to a year, depending on how clearly defined the job is and how clearly it's explained to the new employee.

All the new person's time and attention are absorbed for the first few weeks in learning what's expected. It takes a few days just to find the coffeepot, the cafeteria, and the toilets. After that initial period, as soon as the new employees have some idea of what they are to do and begin to feel that they can do what is expected, their thoughts turn to how well they are doing. Most people do their own performance appraisal at that point.

The real beginning of the new employees' problems, however, is when they look around and try to see what others are doing. Who's in charge here? The minute a new employee begins to analyze, even subconsciously, he or she is involved in the political process. Before that, any political interaction has been defensive, a holding action allowing the employee to find out what was really going on.

This initial entry into the political life of the office begins with the discovery that the lines of authority aren't absolute. It dates from the realization that "something I don't understand or know about is going on here." Elizabeth and Harry expected that their working lives would fit into the patterns they understood. Elizabeth was shocked to find her job in jeopardy for reasons her boss never articulated. Elizabeth focused on the threat and never believed she could reason with her boss or get any kind of explanation.

Harry violated the hierarchy and misjudged his boss's willingness to listen. He insisted on setting his own standard of hard work. Neither Elizabeth nor Harry saw a pattern in what happened in their jobs. As a result, they blamed themselves for not having known something that had never been taught. That is the key.

The tragedy of Elizabeth and Harry is that each of them learned nothing from their first jobs except that office politics exists. That's not enough to save either from a second, third, or fourth mistake. That's why the focus of the rest of this book will be on mastering the tools of political analysis and strategy planning. Otherwise your entire working life will be a "game," the rules of which aren't in Hoyle and that you're ill-equipped to play.

Chapter 2

Tools of Political Analysis—*or* What's the Score?

As we left Harry and Elizabeth in chapter 1, they were poised for further disasters. Neither had a very clear idea of what he or she had learned from the first job, yet both had gone on to a second job. What Harry and Elizabeth needed was a way to analyze power structures in the office. They needed ways to research the people with whom they'd be dealing. Let's look at what both of them should and would have done, had they known how. The key to managing office politics is analysis. Until you have the tools for analyzing what's happening in your work environment, like Harry and Elizabeth, you are a victim.

Most people assume that the power structure is clearly visible. They suppose they know who really counts in the organization and who is clearly a deadweight. After all, surely the person to whom you report has more power than you do. It follows that the boss's boss must have more power than the boss, the president more power than the vice-presidents, and the chairman of the board the most power of all. The answer is an unqualified "sometimes." Power is never evenly spread like peanut butter over an organization. It's more like lumpy oatmeal. That's why we need some tools for measuring where the power is thickest or where there's none at all, only an illusion.

There are five tools every office politician needs whether he or she plans to move ahead in the organization or just stay put. These are (1) a temperature chart that helps you find the hidden power structure; (2) methods for analyzing and classifying other people in the work environment; (3) techniques for building and using all the internal information networks; (4) a work journal for record keeping and self-assessment; and (5) a process of personal distancing, without which the agony of office politics far outweighs the rewards. We'll start with the temperature chart because it supplies the basic information we need before we *do* anything.

DEVELOPING A TEMPERATURE CHART

If you are to control your career and have any impact on the political environment in your organization, you must find out what the real power relationships are. This is something that no one person can tell you because no one person would have thought it necessary to amass all of the information. You must discover the information through research, observation, and informal interviewing. To do anything about your own political situation—even just understand it—you must know what the overall political climate is and what the power relationships are. Whether this process is called a climate survey, a temperature chart, or a clout chart, it is the keystone to managing office politics.

Organization charts are an organization's way of explaining the formal power relationships in that organization. The temperature chart tells where the real information power resides. The simplest organization chart might look like figure 1.

The chart shows titles in ascending order from manager to chairman of the board. Logically, managers are less powerful than vice-presidents, who are less powerful than the president, who is subordinate to the chairman of the board.

If the chart were done as a pyramid, it would show one person at the pinnacle, with increasingly larger groups descending to the base.

The chart makes all those on the same level look as if they had equal rank and power. All vice-presidents appear to be equal. All managers appear the same. This is most unrealistic. Not only are all vice-presidents unlikely to command the same amount of power, but one or more allied together may be more

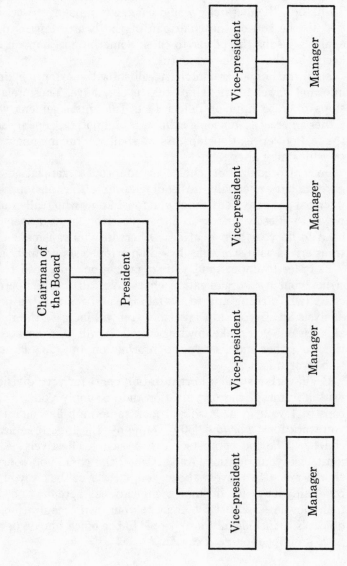

TEMPERATURE CHART
How to Tell Who's Rising and Who's Falling

Fig. 1

powerful than the president or the chairman of the board. One or more may be far less powerful than any one of the managers. Think how the hierarchy would change if a manager were married to the son of the chairman of the board. Power in this analysis means the power to cause something to happen or to keep something from happening.

No formal organization chart will show the extent or kind of informal power relationships that people have. These relationships may be fluid or reflect facts that management would rather ignore. Often people cannot, or will not, talk openly about the real power relationships. As we shall see, talking about relationships may alter them.

Formal organization charts in nonprofit organizations and government are equally misleading because they also mask the informal power system. Since you must know who really has the power to affect your career, either positively or negatively, you need to do your own analysis. Otherwise you can make disastrous errors with strategies based on erroneous information.

In order to understand your organization, you need to construct your own organization chart. We call it a temperature chart (who's rising and who's falling), and it's really a power-analysis kit. If you skip this step, you will increase the risks in all decisions you make down the road. It will take considerable time to gather and classify the information, but it's guaranteed to be worth it.

Begin with a standard organization chart for your division or working unit. If the organization didn't supply you with one, construct your own. It should look something like figure 1. If you work for a *Fortune* "500" company, the total organization chart will be too cumbersome to research effectively. At the most, use your division. At the least, the chart you construct should reach two levels above you, two levels below you, and cover all your peers. In small organizations, there may not be as many levels, so adjust the chart to your own organization. The object is to include all those people in the office who do or could have an impact on your career.

IDENTIFYING AND CLASSIFYING THE PLAYERS

Put the names next to the titles in the boxes. Remember that job titles rarely reflect the real (informal) power structure. They are simply a beginning. Then take a sheet of paper and put on it the name and title of one of the people on your chart. Use a separate sheet of paper for each person. We are now going to put together the information necessary to decide how much power each of these people can actually exercise. There are ten steps to this analysis for each sheet of paper, or person, you have.

1. *To whom does this person report? What is that person's position?*

If vice-president Dan reports to vice-president Laura, Dan is less powerful than Laura and also less powerful than the vice-presidents who report directly to the president. The same is true of a manager or supervisor who reports to another with the same title. Least powerful is the person who, like Gaul, is divided into parts, and is responsible to a different supervisor for each part of his or her job. In fact, that person is in the worst political position of all.

2. *Does this person manage by default, dictatorship, or somewhere in between? What is his or her management style?*

This is very important to later analysis and decision making. At this point, you may jot down some observations about the person's style. Are there any major differences in style from that of others at the same level or above?

3. *Who reviews this person's decisions? Who has the power to veto a decision?*

The power to command is the primary test of overall power. Look very carefully at this. A manager who likes to "touch base" or "check things out" or "bounce ideas off" his boss may be seeking a ratification or review of decisions. This can look like teamwork, rather than lack of command to the trained eye. Try to find out how often and on what kinds of decisions the person "touches base." Look carefully: *Are this person's decisions vetoed regularly?* Of course, it won't be called a veto. It's more likely to come about as "putting off" or "rethinking that decision." Do not be misled. Other people in the organization know that if Joe or Sally always has to "touch base" with the boss on decisions, anyone who needs a quick decision might as well carry the ball directly and get the word from someone who does have the power.

For instance, it's fairly common in businesses with twenty-five to fifty employees for the owner to make all decisions. He or she is wedded to the power of ownership and relishes ratifying each decision. As a result, supervisors, managers, and even vice-presidents are passed over because insiders and outsiders know that only Tom, the owner, can decide.

4. *How much will this person's decisions affect the overall profitability or effectiveness of the organization? of the division? Is this a staff or line position?*

Jobs fall into two categories. There are profit-center jobs (which bring income into the organization) and cost-center jobs (which spend money with no offsetting income). You can tell which people are line people (profit centers) and which are staff people (cost centers). This will vary from organization to organization because it's job situational.

For instance, personnel is a staff position most of the time. In a personnel agency or search firm, however, personnel jobs are line jobs because that's how the organization makes a profit. Line people are power centers more often than staff people because profit is most important. Profit is what the business is all about. The exceptions may be people in staff jobs who provide a service so critical to line people that they have disproportionate power. Some corporate attorneys, research chemists, or information specialists fit this description. The closer Martha is to controlling a profit center, the more power she can be assumed to have. You will want to look at Martha's superiors and subordinates to verify this. Martha may do relatively little and be carried by those above and below her. It's important to know not only how much power she has but also whether she exercises it personally or delegates most of it.

5. *What has this person's promotion record been within the organization?*

If the person has been in the job less than five years, you will want to check around and see what other jobs she or he has had both in your organization and in others. How often has the person moved around within the organization? If the person has managed the same department or function for ten or more years, there is little reason to think that she or he is a mover. This is less true higher up the ladder, though even vice-presidents are moved around. Too many moves can be a negative factor. It may indicate that the person has not done well and is on someone's hit list or is being put in a do-nothing job where she or he can "fade." This is less likely, however, now that mandatory retirement can't be used to prune deadwood, but some organizations retain potential vestiges of this maneuver.

6. *How many and what kinds of people report to this perso.*

Sheer numbers may or may not be important. A person managing two hundred factory workers or two hundred people ‑ word processing is less powerful than a person managir ‑ twenty-five sales representatives. Still, it's important to know how many people report to the person and what those subordinates do. If there are several different levels of people reporting to one person, it's a sign of greater power than if it's just two hundred workers on the same level. Sheer numbers can be important if those workers control an important function. For instance, in a bank the director of operations controls check processing, data processing, and so on, and is very important. In other organizations, operations may be the organization's swamp.

7. *Who of equal rank within the organization consults with the person on that person's decision? How many of these people are there?*

An almost certain sign of power is the person who is consulted by his or her peers for advice, particularly when this advice carries no penalty if it's not taken. Advice is a form of influence if it's taken. A person who appears to be a "sounding board" for peers may actually wield considerable power if people use the advice they get or if it is known that this person is "wise" and a good resource. It's not the power to command but the power to persuade. This kind of person can be very important to your career. Therefore you will want to identify whether or not each person has this kind of power or lacks it.

8. *With whom does this person go to lunch and/or out for a drink?*

The mark of power here is the variety of levels and job titles held by the people with whom this person lunches or socializes or occasionally goes for a drink. The more variety, the more likely that the person is plugged into an assortment of internal information networks. You will want to look carefully at anyone who lunches or drinks with the same person consistently. Lucy and Alice eat lunch together every day. Lucy may like Alice very much on a purely personal level. On the other hand, it may mean that Lucy and Alice are isolated from other peers. Nothing that occurs during or in connection with the business day is or can be purely social.

9. *How astute is this person politically?*

What is your gut reaction to this person? Is he or she liked or disliked? What kind of information comes through the grapevine about him or her? What does his or her secretary say when speaking off the record? This is very important because, as the number of secretaries continues to decline nationally, the remainder become less tolerant of mistreatment and more sensitive to injustice. They will talk about it and in detail as they adjust their résumés.

10. *What is this person's educational and socioeconomic background? What is his or her heritage?*

This is a valuable bit of information and may help explain something that can be explained in no other way. For instance, a Rockefeller scion might be better treated in a particular company, at least at the outset, than his or her talents might warrant. Education may be important if the person is educationally mismatched with others at his or her level. Someone who dropped out of high school may fit comfortably into the sales department but be at odds with the environment of an investment banking firm.

After you have answered these ten questions for the people on your organization chart, you must rank these same people in order of importance disregarding the titles they hold. You will have to make some tight decisions because some of the people may resemble Tweedledum and Tweedledee. In close races, vote for the person with the best promotion record. The slow mover at the same level is almost always less powerful. The myth of the "fast-track" person is very powerful.

WHO'S ALLIED WITH WHOM?

At this point, you're ready to look at another aspect of informal power. On the chart, who is allied with whom? Go back to the chart and draw broken lines between the people who are allies. Your chart should resemble the chart in figure 2.

You will be struck by the fact that people with the least power, as revealed in the first ten steps of your analysis, tend to

TEMPERATURE CHART
How to Tell Who's Rising and Who's Falling

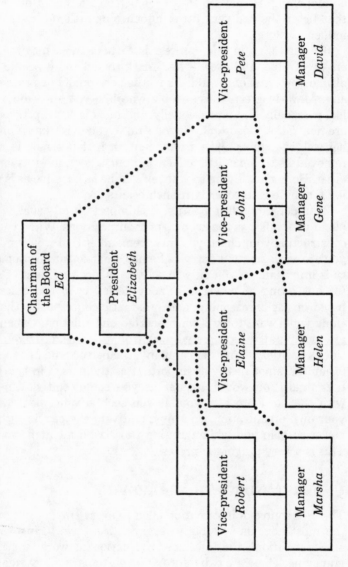

Fig. 2

have fewer allies. In fact, if there are no broken lines coming from or going to one of the boxes, you will want to analyze what is happening. It may be that that person's job is in danger or that he or she has very little influence or little desire to have influence.

The final step in your process is to take three magic markers—red, blue, and green—and mark in red those people who dislike you or whom you dislike either personally or professionally. Mark in green those people who like you and whom you like personally and professionally. In blue, mark the people who are neutral. A person may be neutral if you don't know him or her well enough to make a judgment, or if that person is so far removed as to have little effect on your career one way or the other. Be honest. Lying to yourself will be as effective as is dieting for those who covertly munch éclairs.

To understand office politics, it is important to visualize people in your office as the keepers of their positions. When you are constructing your chart, you must remember that it is not Jerry you are analyzing but Jerry as he fills a particular position. Jerry is important to you only in that he is vice-president of sales (or marketing or whatever). Your decisions in the office are based on logic, reasoning, and pragmatic concerns. So the last thing you'd want to be is warmhearted and emotional when you are looking at the people who control your future. If you consider a position in another company, the person who fills the role of janitor is not nearly as important as the person in charge of personnel. You would, insofar as you could, cultivate people with the power to hire you. If you seek advancement within your own organization, you must cultivate the people with the power to help you while defusing those who might harm you. This is a very pragmatic process.

UNDERSTANDING THE GRAPEVINE

The best source of information open to every employee is one of the most obvious systems in every office, factory, institution, and association—the informal information network, called the grapevine. There are two information systems in every organization, regardless of the size or nature of the product or service. The formal system consists of memos, reports, house organs, and official promulgations. It carries management's view of what is going on within the organization—or at least what management would like the troops to believe is going on. The informal system consists of people talking to one another in the course of the working day. This network carries rumors, trial balloons, and individual perceptions of what participants think is going on.

Whether it's called the information system, the informal network, office gossip, or simply the grapevine, this exchange of organizational intelligence is an important part of office politics. One of the tools you need if you are to be in charge of your career is the information passing through the informal network. You will need to know how the network functions and how to tap into it. This becomes critical when we consider your individual strategy planning. Therefore we need to look at the ways in which people communicate in the office.

People communicate through writing, speaking, and nonverbal body language. Written communication is easiest to misunderstand or even manipulate because it has only one dimension. The words may be open to various interpretations, but the overall message is carried by words only.

Oral communication is richer because of voice, inflection, cadence, and the ways in which words are used to help carry the message. When the nonverbal dimension is added, for example, when you can see the speaker, an additional element helps carry the message. Body language—the way in which the body either supports or denies what the speaker says—is a critical part of the information-gathering process because it is a hundred times harder to control than written or oral communication alone.

Think of the number of times you've been talking on the telephone and made your voice sound warm and enthusiastic when, if the listener had been able to see you, he or she would have known instantly that you were bored, angry, or just in neutral. Masking your real feelings is much more difficult face to face. That's why, when gathering information, trial lawyers, police, spies, and office politicians like to be face to face with their prey. If you are face to face, you can gauge whether you're getting fact or fancy or a mixture of the two. You may catch someone off guard and learn something you never could have discovered any other way.

Advance information is the only power anyone can hope to have because advance information buys lead time. Lead time means time to plan a strategy or to take advantage of any opportunity. Without it, people are shooting in the dark in making career decisions or reacting to changes on the spur of the moment. Because we want "tips," it's worthwhile to look carefully at the elements of the grapevine.

As about office politics, most of us have ambivalent feelings about the grapevine—even the term throws people off track. We hope we're never mentioned unfavorably, but we like to hear everything about people we know. Because the word *grapevine* seems to be a synonym of the word *gossip,* some people pass on nonbusiness-related, personal information. This obscures the fact that most of the information passed through the grapevine tends to be business related.

About 80 percent of the information passed along the grapevine at any one time has some basis in fact. There have been any number of studies that support this figure, as do our own information surveys. Even the most outrageous rumor may have some factual base. Joann may have heard that the company is moving to Peru. It may be that one department is moving to Peru, Illinois. One specific rumor may be false, even deliberately so, but overall there is more fact than imagination in the network. Keep in mind that because the grapevine is spoken rather than written, it's much better at spreading ideas, impressions, and big changes than at carrying details. The bigger and bolder the idea, the more total the change, the more extreme the impression, the more likely it is that the grapevine will have correct information.

Lacking information, some people make up things to fill in gaps and pass their fantasies along as facts. But the reason there is four times as much fact as fantasy in the network is that each person who hears the information decides what and how much to pass on. That means every piece of information is continually scrutinized for each bit of truth and remolded as new facts become available. With that many editors, the truth has a fairly good chance of being identified.

The grapevine will not be able to pick up all intelligence, even though the missing pieces may be very important. If the person who might put the information into circulation controls it exclusively, he or she can decide what will be made available. There are no overall controlling principles for what reaches the network. Thus, much trivia about people's personal lives, new babies, and so on will show up; when there's nothing better to talk about people will discuss trivia, just as they do at dull cocktail parties.

As long as each manager does not type, carry out the boss's orders, or plan things for others to do totally by himself or herself, management cannot stop the informal network. Although such changes would eliminate some players from the network, they would still not stop the continual flow of rumor and fact that spread throughout the organization. Besides, managers need that information as much as the troops.

In order to maximize the usefulness of the network, you will have to identify people who are good sources of information. Good does not mean just reliable. Don't cut yourself off from sources that reflect mood and fantasy as well as reality. Managers often make this mistake of not wanting to listen to the gripes, dreams, and general cud chewing of employees. These raw data are often the harbingers of problems that could surprise the manager down the road.

As with all office politics, there's a lot of barter. All information gathering tends to be a trading process. You are going to have to exchange information if you're to learn anything. Nobody is going to give you a startling rumor in exchange for nothing. People expect to share what you've learned from sources they don't have. The key is to share what you've heard but not what you think it means or what you plan to do about it. You can say you heard that Al is being transferred to Denver without supplying all the scattered information you've heard about the dissolution of Al's department. Or you can say that the department may be phased out without mentioning Al. You don't need to add that you have decided to try to fill the void.

There are many excellent reasons for not sharing your interpretations. The first is that they are highly personal and reflect your own biases and values. Second, if you are planning to move up or merely want to survive where you are, you don't want to signal your strategies via the grapevine until you're ready to take action. That limits their applicability and usefulness to anyone else who might want to ride piggyback on your game plan. Always keep in mind that everything you say is likely to find its way into the rumor mill. That is true whether you're the president of the company or the mail person. The grapevine is very democratic and passes on all kinds of undigested, unverified information regardless of source.

Third, you are in competition with others for power, raises, promotions, transfers, or whatever you've identified as your objectives. (See the next chapter for a full discussion of goal setting.) Why help competitors beat you out (if you have the "right" interpretation of events, for instance)? You can be cooperative and friendly without stoking other people's feelings or giving them ideas.

For example, if you tell John, a fellow manager, that Woody is looking for someone strong on ideas, planning, and analysis and that you plan to apply for the job, John can use that information in two ways. First, he can tell the boss that you're weak in those areas. Second, he can tell the boss that those areas are his forte. You are counting on John to forget his own interests in the name of friendship. This is not a good strategy, and it puts both you and John in a bind. Neither can act decisively careerwise because the friendship is automatically on the line.

The grapevine provides a certain anonymity for the players. It may identify by name the subject of rumors, but it rarely identifies the person or persons who started the rumor. As a result, it's often difficult to identify the people you'd want to include in your own information network. To uncover the most valuable contacts, you'll need to tap several people from each of three sources: secretaries, your organization's competitors, and peers within your own organization. Your boss or someone on his or her level might be included in your network, but it's harder to trade tidbits with someone who has direct power over you.

Secretaries
Secretaries are excellent sources of nonspecific information because they communicate so effectively at a nonverbal level. Who has not seen a secretary rush through the halls to the photocopy machine with a worried expression or stay late many nights in a row only to learn later that a major change was afoot? They often have the inside story on change. It doesn't require Sher-

lock Holmes to put together a secretary's behavior, the nature of the boss's job, and the information in circulation. If you are to excel as an information gatherer, you must learn to be alert to every shade of meaning, every isolated fact, every inexplicable detail. You must become an office data bank.

The most effective way to get specific information from secretaries is to treat them with respect. They are professionals with needs and ambitions of their own. Treat the relationships you build with them as trading relationships between equals. At the top of the chart, the chairman of the board may depend on his or her secretary to take the pulse of the organization. The secretary may be a pipeline to the top. Assume that most secretaries stand well with their bosses. Almost all secretaries can be important allies and sources of information if they choose to be. If not, they can be powerful enemies. A secretary who has decided you're a loser can put that idea into the grapevine over his or her powerful boss's name, and by the time the boss gets into the act and denies it, the damage to your career may have been done.

Some women who have made it in an organization create special problems for themselves. They try to disassociate themselves from secretaries, especially if they were once secretaries themselves. The more recently they've left that role, the harder they try. No matter what her formal rank, any woman may be mistaken for a secretary, so for her to avoid secretaries in order to prevent that possibility offers no solution. The old boys (male peers) are not going to take Mary in willingly and share their intelligence, so she's cut off from that information source. It's shockingly shortsighted of Mary to cut herself off from the secretarial circuit without a substitute information source.

But even secretaries have limits as information sources; some may feel a need to protect their bosses. This loyalty may be superseded by loyalty to the organization or by your ability to persuade them that you are helping their bosses even though it may not appear that way. Even a secretary who treats everything as confidential can help by giving hints and nonverbal clues if you are thought to be deserving. If the boss has a hangover on Monday morning and you're bursting to tell him or her your great idea, the secretary can save you and the idea by suggesting 2:00 P.M. for the historic confrontation rather than 10:00 A.M. This may prevent your plan from being shot down.

Outside Competitors

A second group of sources that you need to cultivate are your organization's competitors. This has two advantages. First, very few other people in your own organization will think of this, so you'll generally have more complete information than they do. Second, you will be tapping a completely different source of information.

Who could possibly be more interested in gossip about Xerox than the people in the photocopy equipment division of IBM? Officially, IBM and Xerox would have to deny that their salespeople, programmers, secretaries, or any other kind of employee regularly cross-pollinated with their competitors' employees. It would be serious if these people were exchanging trade secrets. They are not. Political rumors are largely uncontrolled anyway. No intelligent employee would trade confidential information. It's dangerous and unethical. The kind of thing we have in mind is rumors of who's getting fired or promoted or transferred in your company, thereby creating a possible opening for you.

Each of us belongs to both a business and a social network. These two networks are not entirely separate, and people cross from one to the other. You meet people socially and in professional or union meetings and talk business. For instance, if you worked for Ford and met Buick people at trade meetings, you'd both have an interest in trading what you'd heard about the other's organization. What Ford people would identify as important in the political situation at Buick would be different from what Buick employees would identify as such. This adds a new dimension to your overall picture of what's happening in your own office. If Buick thinks you at Ford should be concerned about Joe's drinking and Pete's behavior on sales trips, maybe you should get more information in that area. If your competitor asks whether a particular rumor is true and you haven't heard the rumor, you'll want to check it out.

Peers Within Your Own Organization

Your peers in your company, who are also competitors, are important sources of information, provided that you analyze what is not said as well as what is said. That is, if you hear rumors from your secretarial vine and hear an approximation from competitors but nothing from your peers, you have learned that your peers aren't talking, and that fact may be even be more important to you. A sure sign that your career is in trouble is the drying up of your internal sources of information. All of a sudden you are isolated. The only news you get is written and has been given to everybody else as well.

Because you and those on your level may be in head-on competition for promotion, your relationships with them will be different from those with other information sources. You will be expected not only to trade rumors one for one but to trade rumors of like values. It's unlikely you'll be able to get a peer to ante up a major rumor in exchange for one relating to a possibility that would make little difference to either of you.

If there are more than three people on your level, you're bound to find someone who won't exchange information with you. This person is generally from the school that says that gossip is bad and a person should "keep his or her own counsel." Unless you are altruistic, do not feed this person information in return for nothing. People have to be taught to play the game, however tough the learning process may be. Nobody should expect a news digest for free. But that person's secretary and the people in his or her grapevine should be cultivated.

A good basic rule to follow is never to offer a peer information that you would not want to see hand-lettered on your office wall. But what should you do about information you believe is highly confidential? First, there's much less of this than most people believe. It's highly unlikely that a person high enough on the chart to make things happen would do so without anyone else having input into or knowledge of the process. If you are a recipient of information that you know is unknown to more than one or two other people and you have been sworn to secrecy, you are ethically bound to respect that trust. If you don't, not only will the people who are involved know that you are a fink, but other sources of information you value will also dry up.

Once you have plugged yourself into the internal network and your resource people are in place, what kind of information should you seek? Your goal is to learn about any changes in the organization or its personnel that might affect your career and to do so far enough in advance to protect your own interests. Unless something catastrophic is happening in your organization—such as an unfriendly buy-out attempt or an IRS audit by special agents—the place to start is with the past.

Get an oral history à la *Roots* of top management. Never mind what the public relations department lays on the media. The people who saw present management ascend can offer excellent insight into that process.

For instance, if you are in data processing and you are determined to be president of the company someday, you'd want to know how possible that really was before you devoted twenty years of your life to the project. If you have built your personal network effectively, you should be able to send out a question and get back information. This is informal interviewing, a very casual but important part of information gathering. Suppose you want to know how anyone could expect to rise to the top. How did the president get there? What was his or her career path? Your sources question their sources, and the word comes back that nobody in the past forty years has risen above the vice-presidential level except people from sales. In fact, you learn from other sources that three of five of the current vice-presidents started in sales. Your boss's boss, who is head of management information systems (formerly called data processing), started in sales. So if you have no interest in sales, you may want to reconsider your ambition vis-à-vis your present employer. You may want to consider another company in which data-processing people have moved further up the ladder.

The single greatest mistake any worker can make is to cut himself or herself off from a variety of sources of information in favor of one or two. Although few people would plan to do this, they may accomplish the same thing by having coffee, lunch, or drinks with the same people month after month. Martha and Michael ate together every day. In so doing, they limited themselves to a dangerously incomplete set of facts and speculations. You can test yourself to see if you are cut off from sources of information you should be plugged into by answering the question, "What has happened in my organization within the last month that surprised me?" If you can point out any major event—someone's leaving, promotion, or termination; a new policy announcement; an acquisition or merger in the works— you are sadly out of touch with the power and information sources in your organization.

It may be you'd rather not know in advance of any impending

disasters in your office or career. That's pretty shortsighted. Nothing is ever final until it is official, and you might manage things with some advance notice. Again, the only power you can hope to have in most situations is the power to prepare in advance because you knew that a particular change was at hand. Without the lead time to plan a response, protect your career, or seize an opportunity to apply for a job about to be vacated, you are a luckless victim, and as surprised as anybody else at what happens.

WORK JOURNAL

When we talked about performance appraisal in chapter 1, we lamented the lack of control the ordinary person has over this important part of his or her career. One of the tools you need is a way to counter the office's performance appraisal with information of your own. The tool you need is the work journal or record of the achievements of your career.

People rarely get a chance to prove their competence once and for all. With a work journal, if you are challenged, you're prepared. An added bonus of the work journal is that it boosts your ego because you see what you are accomplishing. There is no way to give yourself your own strokes without written records.

The work journal idea was introduced by John Crystal and Richard Nelson Bolles in the book *Where Do I Go from Here with the Rest of My Life?* (Berkeley, Calif.: Ten Speed Press, 1977). The purpose they saw was to help negotiate raises and promotions at performance appraisals. They also saw this as a tool for setting benchmarks in a person's career.

The work journal, which must be kept faithfully, at least biweekly, is a comprehensive record of what you do on the job. This includes what you've produced, regardless of how that's measured; any of your ideas that have been implemented; positive feedback and ego strokes you've received for your work; and specific details of ways you've helped the organization or department save or make money, cut costs, solve problems, or improve efficiency.

Unless you keep the work journal on a regular basis, it will be too incomplete to be worth anything to you. The idea is to be as complete as possible. You need not only written notes   at you've done but samples of your work as well. These samples may include memos to and from others, reports, proposals, and publicity clips—in other words, anything that shows what you have done.

Most working people depend on the organization to keep records of what they do. This is bad strategy because it puts control in someone else's hands. A very common misconception is that the organization keeps concise, complete records. This is rarely true. Your boss may remember when you made a mistake, but even that is rarely written. Consequently, he or she has an *overall* impression rather than specifics.

No system of record keeping is infallible, but without your own written records you will always be in the position of accepting someone else's version of the facts. Kennedy's Law is that this version will never be the one you would want to be the "official" one.

The single most valuable characteristic of the work journal is that it provides a benchmark. It lets you measure your progress. If your work journal reads pretty much the same year after year, you can be fairly sure you're not progressing. The journal also provides a benchmark that allows you to compare where you're going with where people above you on the ladder are headed. How similar are your backgrounds? What gaps stand out in yours?

Keeping careful records makes it much more difficult to kid or just plain delude yourself about what's happening. You'll buy fewer promises from bosses about "waiting it out" or "trying to get you that promotion." It's easy to buy those promises when you have no record of how many times the boss has played that tune before. You may still decide to stay and wait for the promise to materialize, but at least you'll have made a choice and not just drifted into the decision.

The work journal helps you evaluate and put into perspective the boss's analysis of your work. If you and the boss see your work in vastly different ways and have different values about what you've done, you can compare the two versions and decide who's kidding whom. It may be that you hadn't realized how very biased your boss is on certain topics (not necessarily a sex bias; it may be a matter of life-style or personality). If so, you may need to confront the fact that he or she is never going to value your performance very highly. This may mean getting a better job somewhere else with a boss who has different and more compatible biases.

People talk about salary negotiation as if it were really a negotiating process. If you listen in on two people doing it, however, it doesn't sound as if they're negotiating. It sounds as if one person is giving something to another.

BOSS: Well, Mary, it's been another year.
MARY: Yes, it has.
BOSS: How does 7 percent sound to you?
MARY: Fine.
BOSS: Good. Well, see you next year.

Mary is going to have a problem if she wants more than that 7 percent. She's going to have to come up with convincing evidence that she's earned it. After waiting all year to go from $20,000 to $25,000, Mary is going to be sorely disappointed with her paltry raise. She will have to accept it, though, if she can't demonstrate very convincingly that she's worth more. Without the work journal she doesn't have a chance. All she can do is talk vaguely about what she's done. It's got to be vague—no evidence! How much more effective to bring in written records and documents to support her claim. Even if she is refused, her boss will know that she is serious, prepared, and professional. For Mary, if her argument doesn't work on her current boss, there's always the option of trying the same material on someone else.

Finally, the work journal will help in preparing the next résumé. Most people sweat bullets when they have to write a résumé. They spend hours trying to remember exactly what they were doing three years ago or five years ago, or even ten years ago. They have difficulty defining what they really do. Could you summarize your job—and what you've accomplished—in five sentences?

The work journal makes it much easier to pick out your sterling successes and highlight them on the résumé. It assures that there will be no gaps caused by not being able to remember what you did. Instead of feeling dissatisfied with a résumé that took you two days to put together, you can use the material from your work journal and spend your time polishing and editing instead of searching your memory for information.

Keeping a journal is neither difficult nor time-consuming. You may want to take ten minutes every Friday afternoon and jot notes on what you've done that week and the status of your projects. At least once every other week, look over what you've written and be sure you still understand your notes. Every three months summarize all of your notes into one page of readable information that shows what you have contributed. Whether you keep your raw data in a spiral-bound notebook, on three-by-five cards, on the back of the envelope your paycheck comes in, or any other way, the important thing is to do this regularly.

Sample Entries in the Work Journal

Remember that as you keep your work journal, you are looking for ways you have helped the company: cut costs, improved procedures, developed new ideas, improved morale, improved profitability, and so on. Not everything any one employee does is going to be earthshaking. Not every individual employee can pull the company back from the brink, invent nylon, or spread sunshine. We are looking for genuine contributions you made, even though you regard them as modest. Do not undervalue what you have done. Chair fillers abound, and the fact that you are doing things should be recorded. This raw data can be used both in seeking promotion and in changing jobs and careers. It is politically very important.

With these caveats in mind, here are some sample work journal entries. Each is a summary, though the individual in each case would keep samples of all supporting data.

Editor, company newsletter with a circulation of 7,500

Cut costs in publishing the newsletter by 10 percent over a six-month period through:

a. Researching a less expensive paper stock that looked comparable to the old stock;
b. Using an IBM Variable Space typewriter for producing copy rather than having it typeset at $37.50 per hour;
c. Better writing and editing to reduce bulk by 20 percent without sacrificing the quality and quantity of news the paper carried.

Dollar savings: $1,600 per month for each of the last six months for a total savings of $9,600.

Cost accountant for manufacturing firm

1. Developed a mechanized cost system to replace a manual system. By using computer for system, saved 35 percent in manpower costs and reduced by 20 percent the time from input to output of information.

2. Developed new ways to relate costs to sales, which resulted in quicker information to top management so that sales lags would be immediately apparent.

Savings of $800 per month resulted from the first change. Total savings over six-month period: $4,800.

Stick to demonstrable facts as much as you can. When in doubt, give reasonable estimates. Summarize on a three-month basis. If you scribble notes between six-month reports, be sure that you transcribe them carefully. Memory does funny things, and many a good idea may go unreported. Careful note-keeping is essential.

PERSONAL DISTANCING

The final tool you need before you take any action is a tool for protecting yourself from the pain, frustration, and personal barbs of the political process. People who want to withdraw from the push and shove of office politics tend to be pain avoiders, and nobody can fault them for that! Still, since office politics is going on whether we want to avoid it or not, we need a tool to reduce at least some of the pain and to protect our egos from as many barbs as possible.

In theory, we are all professional people. We're trying to do our jobs as best we can and take pride in the quality of our work. Whether we rivet auto-body frames or direct corporations, we need to have an attitude of professionalism about our work. In fact, most of us are deeply, emotionally involved not only with what we do but in the way we do it and the people with whom we do it. This involvement causes problems and doesn't guarantee that the work production will be of a higher quality. It makes people vulnerable by involving the ego. (We use the term *ego* to mean your sensitive feelings—the things that hurt or elate you.) It is hard to do a good job while trying to get one's ego stroked or to prevent it from being bruised.

You need a tool to protect your ego in order to be more professional on the job. That tool is personal distancing. It allows you to disengage your ego and therefore makes you less vulnerable. The result is greater productivity and less pain.

Personal distancing means saying to yourself that there are actually two of you: a professional working self and a personal self. You are going to put some emotional space between you the working professional and you the human being. That space is going to be the buffer zone that protects your ego and lets you do the best job possible with the least political pain. The rallying cry of people who practice personal distancing is, "These people are responding to the professional me. They don't know the real me well enough to dislike it. Therefore I'm not going to take it personally."

After all, if you left your house one morning and were mugged in the street, you would not think the mugger had looked up your name in the telephone book and picked you personally for that experience. You would think you'd had the misfortune to be in the wrong place at the wrong time. The same is true of office politics. If you are "mugged," used, or victimized in the office, it will be less painful all around if you do not personalize the experience.

Personal distancing means that you look at the event as a factor in the dynamics of the office. This doesn't mean that you don't feel pain, get mad, or attempt to get even. But it does mean that you attempt to handle it professionally, without overreacting on the spot.

It exhausts people to put their egos on the line in every confrontation at work. It leaves them burned out and difficult for others to deal with. Everybody else sees the person's problem and tries to tiptoe around his or her ego. This forces people to use energy and time in a manner that is not productive. They will eventually resent you for that. Besides, it's up to you to protect yourself emotionally. If you don't, who will?

Distancing yourself certainly doesn't mean being withdrawn and uncaring. Certainly, professionals in every line of work care about the people they work with and for, the quality of work they do, and the impact that that work has on the organization.

Actors have always practiced a form of distancing in their work. When a movie or stage star plays a role, the actor or actress sees criticism of himself or herself as criticism of the way the role was played, not of the player personally. Otherwise there would be far fewer actors and actresses! Many actors and actresses depersonalize even *personal* criticism on the theory that personalizing work is the critic's problem and not theirs. (A very sensible, if difficult to implement, position.)

You can learn, just as actors and actresses do, to distance yourself in order to protect your ego. This requires the same kind of practice and concentrated learning as would any other new skill, but it will be *well worth your time*. You will probably always respond at gut level to criticism as a personal attack, but you will distance yourself both in the way you look at things later and in the way you respond on the spot.

The first step is to remind yourself every morning before you leave home that you are locking your ego in a jar and leaving it there until you return. Unless you think about this consciously, it will be difficult to remind yourself later in the day that you are operating exclusively in your professional mode.

Second, you must tell yourself that you are a professional at whatever you do. You work for the organization because it pays you. This is difficult for people who personalize what they do to the point that they go around telling people, "I love what I do so much, I'd do it even if I didn't get paid." If you say that long enough, someone may take you seriously. Don't. Tell yourself that your role here is to earn at least whatever you are paid.

Third, you must tell yourself that criticism of yourself is really criticism of your work, not criticism of you as a person. The fact that someone criticizes your work as if he or she were criticizing you as a person is his or her problem. Such utter lack of diplomacy is going to get the person in the end anyway.

Finally, nothing is personal even if it's good. Not personalizing failure or criticism also means not personalizing success. If you fall out of your professional mode even for a minute, you'll be lost. It's only a short step from there back to personalizing criticism.

In addition to keeping you mentally healthy and reasonably

content in your job, the process of distancing has advantages in your relationships with people who work with you. Distancing helps keep you from brutality and petty revenge because it's out of role, if not out of character. It reduces the pain you inflict on others because you'll be less likely to criticize them personally when you're trying so hard to control that distancing in your own work life. You won't tell Phil that he is stupid; you will say that you found the reasoning in his report unconvincing or somewhat unorganized. You won't say that Jim is a bozo who can't cross a street without being hit by a car; you'll ask him why he comes in late on a daily basis.

Distancing makes it easier for others to work with you. Your boss sees you as someone who's in control, not as a harried emotional wreck. This has got to improve your prospects even if the boss himself is harried and emotional. People who are perpetually upset tend to dislike working with others of the same ilk.

Distancing makes objectivity easier because you have removed yourself emotionally from the fray. It won't still your conscience, however. People's values tend to break through any kind of process.

Finally, distancing will tend to make you less self-conscious. Shy actors can be very bold when playing a part. You'll feel less shy speaking up in meetings and working through political thickets because you'll know it's not the real you—it's the professional you—who's on stage doing your job. And don't kid yourself—working in an office is a constant performance.

Chapter 3

Setting Objectives and Goals—*or* What's It All Worth?

In the past five years it has become very chic to talk about career planning and career goals. Most people can't define a career goal. They know that, like free enterprise and wedded bliss, it's something they should have. Even the people who couldn't distinguish between career goals and career fantasies if one or the other kicked them will talk glibly about their long-range goals.

Ignoring the popular hype, there are five compelling, pragmatic reasons for having both political and career goals. First, both affect your participation in office politics. If you have neither political nor career goals, you're just working at your present job until something better seeks you out or someone better pushes you out. As a passive participant, you don't really need the analysis and techniques laid out in this book. You have no place to go and may not really appreciate where you are. You are not taking charge of your career, only reacting to the strategies of others. As we've said before, no one is going to force you to manage your career. In fact, this whole discussion will just make you feel as guilty as the three-hundred-pound man reading about fasting.

Second, it is only worthwhile to research, plan, and carry out strategies if that effort is directed toward a long-term goal with short-term objectives along the way. It is more efficient to use your energies working toward something that you want to achieve than to go through the motions without thinking about what you are doing or where you are going. In this way, too, wasted energy is at a minimum.

Third, goals provide the long-term meaning and motivation in your work life. There are too many ways people can make enough money just to get by without having to think very hard or very often. To give work meaning over the long run, it is extremely important to have goals. Meaning in work has become increasingly necessary and popular. Objectives provide the benchmarks in reaching goals. If you set neither, you'll never have to worry about not meeting them. This will be restful and nonproductive.

Fourth, if you do nothing over long periods of time, or if what you do isn't directed toward anything specific, you won't be bothered by the guilt feelings that bother others. You won't have to worry or regret not achieving or accomplishing anything. You can kid yourself indefinitely until the day you wake up and find yourself either out of a job or uncomfortable with the one you have. For example, if you want to know if management is serious about its promises for promotion, set a time frame and measure your performance and the promises during that period. If you decide that the organization should make good on its promise of a promotion in eighteen months and twenty months pass, at least you'll be motivated to find out what's happening. You'll have an objective standard by which to evaluate the progress in your career, and you can feel that you are working toward something specific.

Finally, setting goals and objectives is essential to measuring the risks of both career strategies and political strategies. It's simple enough to see why you need objectives and goals to assess the risks of any strategy. After all, without them, the risk could be at any level from none at all to sudden dismissal. Unless you assess the risk and decide whether your strategy is worth it, you'll never know whether you're in control and making intelligent choices or if you're just reacting to the politics in the office and to the paths you see others taking. Borrowing someone else's career plan is about as wise and comfortable as borrowing someone else's toothbrush.

RABBITS IN THE RACE

Before you begin setting goals and objectives, you need to define them. Goals are long-term plans; objectives are short-term plans. Objectives can be met in a specific period of time and are a means to reaching goals. Goals may or may not be reached in a lifetime.

Imagine that you are a greyhound in a race. In order to motivate you, the organizers have a mechanical rabbit that they will let you see but not reach. During the race you will never—no matter how fast you run—get your jaws on that rabbit. Every race you run will have the same rabbit, but you will never get it. Instead, at the end of the race, you know that you will get rest, food, water, and prizes.

In our example, the rabbit represents a goal. It is long-term and unreachable, an incentive to keep you on track. On the other hand, objectives are like individual races. They can be met within a specific time frame. At the end, you get rest, water, prizes, and food.

It's important to distinguish between objectives and goals. You need both, and you need to consider both over a period of time. If you don't, you will set goals that will leave you wondering what to do next. It is important always to have something to strive for because it keeps you on the track and keeps you going. We worked with a man whose goal was to become a millionaire before he reached forty. He saw that as his lifetime goal and never considered what would happen if he reached his goal. What would he do next? As it happened, through an invention he became a millionaire in his mid-thirties. He spent the next fifteen years trying to figure out what to do. He was too young to retire, but he couldn't focus on any activity, work or otherwise, that excited him enough to get him moving again. It took him fifteen years to find another long-term goal.

You are going to have problems if the only career goals you set are really career objectives. For instance, suppose that you hope to use the techniques outlined in this book to help you get promoted to manager. If you set that as your career goal rather than as a short-term objective, you will be in the same boat as our millionaire. What will you do next? It does not follow that someone reaching a goal (even an artificial one) is motivated to just raise his or her sights. That's one of the reasons dollar goals are not really useful—especially during inflationary periods. If it took you a great deal of effort, time, and concentration to get to your goal, the natural tendency is to want to stop, reassess, and look around for a new challenge. Confusing objectives with goals makes the career path a bumpy road of starts, stops, and detours. Planning to become a manager and having it happen provokes a major rethinking. There is not the smooth transition up the ladder that there would be had your goal been to rise as high as you could in the organization. Then being named a manager would have been one objective on the path.

In office politics, a reasonable goal may be to establish excellent working relationships with all senior executives, your peers, and your subordinates. Obviously, this will support your career goal. You won't achieve this 100 percent of the time, and you must think of it as long term. This keeps you from losing perspective and indulging that one mad impulsive urge to get even when someone steps on your toes. Within this overall goal, you will need to set specific objectives that may include pleasing your superior, getting a promotion or transfer, or even just a great recommendation for a new job. Another long-term goal might be to change the way people get elected to public office. You probably will never see a 100 percent change, but you will be able to set and reach many short-term objectives.

Political objectives must be compatible with your career goals and life-style. It is not a good idea to set as your objective advancement to vice-president in a company that values the seventy-hour workweek when you find the forty-hour workweek a strain. Your life-style is probably not going to change dramatically, though you might change parts of it over a period of years. The change would have to reflect a change in your thinking, or else, like holding your breath, it would be temporary. We find that life-styles change goals and objectives, not the other way around. A woman or man who has two small children she or he wants to be with will not work a seventy-hour week short of the threat of starvation. But the same person might embrace the seventy-hour week without a single regret when those two children go away to school.

Office politics is a tool for reaching objectives and goals. It is not an end in itself but a means to an end. "Playing" politics for fun is not only incredibly time-consuming but highly stressful. If you're just trying to amass power for its own sake, how will you know when you have enough? You will also arouse powerful enemies who will see your efforts as destructive to productivity and the work environment. There is a myth to the effect that the people who play politics openly are unethical and probably unproductive, as discussed in chapter 1. That doesn't mean you can't or shouldn't—simply that the price may be high.

For instance, if Janet is seen by her office mates as a brown-nose, constantly stroking her boss and everyone else above her in the hierarchy, her peers will find a way to bring her to heel. If that proves difficult for them to do—let's say that Janet is very careful—they will simply cut her off from the internal networks. That remains the ultimate deterrent because, if she is isolated, she'll not be able to act or react politically as she should.

What kinds of goals and objectives will you set? The easiest approach is to ask yourself what you'd like to be doing at the time you retire. (If you never plan to retire, let's say when they carry you out.) This would be a goal to shoot for. If you are between twenty-two and thirty-five, this is probably too long a period of time, so ask yourself what you'd like to be doing in twenty to thirty years. Then ask about the next fifteen years after that. This may seem like a very long time, but people so frequently underestimate how fast, or how often, they'll move in just five years. They need the longer time frame for planning seven to ten moves.

Go over the research you did in chapter 1. It's possible that you really don't know enough about your present organization or yourself to set a long-term goal. On the other hand, one of the people on your temperature chart may have followed a career path that interests you enough to investigate. Whether your goal is to remain with your present firm for a lifetime or to move on, you should start where you are. Your research may have turned up a number of interesting jobs that you might want to explore. Before you set an objective to get one of those jobs or set a long-term goal to become president of the organization, you will want to know how many people have had approximately the same objectives and goals and what has become of them. One of the benefits of personnel and public relations departments is that both have chronicled the paths to the top of everybody in top management. That's the stuff of press releases to community organizations and introductions to speeches.

Let's suppose that you are now a supervisor in word processing for a bank and looking at the job of vice-president of operations. You go back to the temperature chart and research data and find that the current vice-president started in data processing. He was a programmer for four years, a supervisor in data processing for four years, manager of management information systems for seven years, and has been vice-president of operations for the past five years. He is now forty-five years old. You are twenty-seven. There are two things to be considered. How probable is it that a vice-president will come out of word processing rather than data processing? Will there be a likelihood of an opening with that bank when you are ready for the job?

Suppose you decide the answer is yes to both questions. Then and only then will you be ready to set some goals and objectives in your current setting, which will involve you in office politics as a dynamic rather than static participant. Most people, until they have goals and objectives, are static, that is, defensive players. They are playing to keep what they have rather than to change or increase the job or the amount of power they currently exercise.

Since it's impossible to separate career goals from political goals, it's important to make them compatible from the start. Let's return to Arlene, the word-processing supervisor. Her goal is to move as fast and far as she can. Once she has set her objective to become vice-president, Arlene must research what part political skills played in the current job occupant's rise. In addition to charting that person's career path, she needs to study his or her political path. Arlene can't copy the vice-president's career path exactly. She can only learn some of the moves he or she made and evaluate whether they'd be useful or possible for her. To do this, she turns to the informal information network.

Of course, she could go directly to the vice-president and ask for a summary of his or her political career. But it would be a major waste of time if, like most people, he or she talked about hard work, being in the right place at the right time, and so on. People tend to reconstruct the facts to fit what they wished had happened rather than what actually did happen. The company old-timers, however, will remember the vice-president's failures as well as successes. She should talk to them. It's highly unlikely that a person will report the political errors that he or she has made, but peers will both remember and share.

Suppose that your own situation is vastly different. Perhaps the ultimate job you want has never been filled by someone like yourself. Maybe it's so newly created it has no history, or perhaps the organization is brand new. Maybe you yourself have created the job. In any case, you still don't strike out cold; you look for help from your competitors. Whether you work for a social service agency or General Motors, you have competitors— and thank heaven for that. Without competitors to share the process of learning things the hard way, to make your mistakes for you, every organization would have to make each mistake individually. That would take years and would be like living in the business equivalent of the Stone Age.

Instead, we build contacts with our competitors so that we can tap into their informal information networks. Trade and professional organizations are a major source because they bring people from a variety of organizations together to talk shop. Never undervalue the commuter cocktail hour at such meetings. Whether you're drinking Bloody or Virgin Marys, keep your eyes and ears open. That's when you can do your most effective intelligence gathering. When you find someone who works for a competitor, ask about the person who holds the job you'd like in your own organization. If you need even more basic information, you can find out who does what you'd like to do and how he or she got there. You are not interested in trade secrets but job identification. Most often your initial contact won't be able to provide in-depth information. He or she will, however, be able to pass you on to someone who can. This sort of research is essential to intelligent decision making and always precedes any attempt at strategy planning. Otherwise you'll end up changing strategies under stress because some unexpected but easily anticipated emergency arises. This will enormously increase the wear and tear on you.

For instance, if your long-term goal is a top management job in a particular industry, your organization's place within that industry may be critical. Is the company growing? Where does it stand in relation to its competitors? Are competitors imitating what your organization is doing or vice versa? There are dozens of questions you'll want to look at before you decide to plunge into the office politics involved in a strategy. Your company will not give out that information even through the informal information system because, unless they cross-pollinate with their competitors, they won't have it.

The business and trade press will be important sources of some of this information. Their information will be more accurate and less speculative than what is being said on the street, though less timely, but both kinds of information are important. Street talk is always fresher.

Once you've identified the job in the competitor's organization that you want in your own, determine how that occupant got there. You can transfer the information to your own company or organization. The information is adaptable. As long as the organizations are structured in the same way and/or make or do the same sort of thing, career paths and political information transfer easily from organization to organization, from a business firm to a nonprofit organization. For instance, the organization of a public relations agency and a public relations department of similar size will tend to be similar. The people they hire will tend to have similar career paths.

Thus far we've talked about setting goals and objectives and reality testing them through research both internally and externally. This assumes that you have everything to gain and nothing to lose. We now move on to another kind of reality testing—putting a price on one's goals.

RISK ASSESSMENT

While it's nice to blue-sky about goals, it's important to bring them back to earth through a cost-effort analysis. That means examining what the cost is in terms of effort, cash outlay, and the trade-offs of other things you could be doing with the same resources. Summed up, we call this cost-effort analysis the process of assessing risk.

Simply defined, risk is the chance that something will or will not happen. There are absolute risks that affect everybody across the board. For instance, if you leap from a bridge, there is a knowable risk that you'll fall. There is a knowable risk that you'll live or die as a result of the fall. The same is true of the risk to a child chasing a ball into a street. It can be researched and calculated with a fair degree of accuracy.

But the word *risk* should not connote an automatic negative. If you hand in a report, there is a risk involved. The risk can be good or bad. Your report can reflect how little or how much you know. You can be recognized as a particularly astute or extraordinarily stupid employee.

Career and political risks are not as easily measurable as physical risks for two reasons. First, you make every risk analysis through a screen of your own values; all risk assessment is influenced by personal judgment. Second, other people's behavior is more erratic and less predictable than physical forces; your actions interacting with the actions of others make the outcome less predictable. Even given these two handicaps, we can calculate the risk of any career or political action involving the goals, objectives, and strategy planning we will discuss in the next chapter.

Each risk can be analyzed in terms of probability, cost, and motive. We can assess the *probability* that something will or will not happen. We can assess the probable *cost* in money, time, physical or mental effort, and trade-offs (giving up doing one thing in order to do another). Finally, we can assess the *motive* for the risk. We are taking either a passive risk, a chance taken so we won't lose something, or an active risk, a chance taken so that we will gain something. All three factors are important in risk analysis, but the third measure, motive, is often overlooked because, as we shall see, it seems both obvious and irrelevant.

There is no magic to risk analysis. The people in Las Vegas are doing some fairly sophisticated number crunching to keep the gambling operations profitable. But unlike a roll of the dice, we won't have to bet everything at any one time on the outcome. We can change predictions and levels of risk as we go along.

Suppose that your boss announces an opening for which someone with your skills, educational background, and experience is needed. The person to be hired would do roughly what you do. (This, of course, is rarely the case, but we want to walk through a fairly simple example until we get the hang of risk analysis.) You know someone, Perry, who would seem qualified for the job on the basis of the information you have. Before you check further into Perry's suitability for the job—much less mention his name—you must assess the political risks as follows:

1. What is the probability that Perry meets your boss's requirements? What is the probability that Perry and the boss would be compatible? What is the probability that if you recommended someone who later proved a failure, the boss would hold this against you? What is the probability that the boss would hire Perry if he presented himself as a candidate? Depending on the boss's personality, values, and temperament, you can develop other risk issues.

2. What is the cost of your recommendation? Are there money costs? Will you have to buy Perry lunch to tell him about the job? Will the recommendation cost time if you have to get more information from or about Perry? Will that time be on your own or during the working day? How much time would you estimate your research will take? Will you be expected to meet with Perry before he is presented to the boss? In other words, will you have to prescreen? How much physical and mental effort will be involved in presenting Perry? Will Perry make demands that will require this kind of effort? If so, how much effort will you need to expend? What will you have to give up that you could or should be doing in order to follow through with this recommendation? If you do make the recommendation, what are the trade-offs in terms of time expended that might have been used playing tennis, advancing your own goals, or in other productive ways? If Perry isn't the best candidate, will you be expected to produce another suitable one?

3. What is your motive in making the recommendation? Are you hoping to gain some political advantage because you are helpful, or are you hoping to hold on to some advantage or goodwill you've already built up? What are the risks that the hiring of your candidate would affect your present position? Would it be an active change for good or a neutral change, neither bad nor good, or could it possibly even adversely affect your career?

Naturally, you will not go through such an elaborate analysis on every single political decision. You will, however, want to develop your own checklist for analyzing risks in any situation that takes into account your boss's nature and the values of your boss's boss. Once you've worked out the risk issues, this will take a tenth the time to do that it took to read about. These are the hot buttons that must be considered before you make a decision that affects your position in either your work environment or vis-à-vis your boss and his or her boss.

You are not making an intelligent decision unless you go

through this process. You're shooting from the hip. Even if you are a political gunslinger of considerable skill, there are some decisions that are too important for such casual treatment. For instance, it's not smart to decide whether to accept or reject a promotion on the basis of your gut response alone. While ordinarily you'd analyze the risk in your mind without writing a research paper, when you're considering a promotion, it's worth the extra time to write things down. Writing is very different from, and somehow more important than, any mental exercise.

Writing things down helps people get more comfortable with risk analysis, especially if they practice first on inconsequential decisions. If I eat two bags of potato chips, what is the chance I'll gain weight? What is the cost of eating those chips? Am I risking the extra calories to hold on to or to gain something? A second example would be, Should I go to the water cooler for another drink of water? Will it mean I may miss a phone call? Will it refresh me so much that I am able to think more clearly? Am I risking the time it takes to go to the water cooler in order to hold on to or to gain something?

Most people do some kind of risk analysis instinctively, but they just don't think of it as risk analysis. The only reason we formalize the process is to flag its importance to politics. But there is a danger. Instead of risk analysis making people more prudent and inclined to think through the issues, a great many have an attack of brinksmanship. They decide to see how close they can come to getting fired without actually having it happen. Political risk can't be measured precisely enough to help people who want to risk their jobs in one reckless, soul-satisfying act.

So far we've talked about measuring the risk of doing something. Jack saw office politics as a game and his boss as a boob. The more he analyzed what his boss did (very little) and how effectively (not very), he began to bait the boss. He forgot in his exuberance that the boss still had the power to cause him a lot of trouble, even bounce him out of the organization. Jack's fate was to be transferred within the organization after a particularly nasty row with the boss. Analysis doesn't mean that once you've discovered that you're working for the criminally bewildered, you should let them know your opinion. That's both bad manners and terrible politics. We now turn to the risks of the status quo.

Making *no* decision is a political decision because taking no action is as risky as taking any particular action could be. Sitting on dead center and refusing to move has enormous hidden risks. The political killers are the "shoulds," the procrastination that ends in political devastation. For example, how do you measure the risks of devoting lunch hours to shopping, going to art museums, or playing racquetball with someone outside the business who cannot be useful to your career politically or professionally? It could clear your mind and refresh you for the afternoon. Deep in your heart, though, you know you should be making political contacts and working to advance your career. The alternative might be using that time for building internal information networks. If you've been treating lunch hours as R & R—and your career hasn't stalled or you haven't been fired— you can still change. In most people's working lives there are few definitive decisions that can't be adjusted or even changed entirely. If you have been backpedaling politically, you can alter your level of participation at any time.

Some people are so turned off by office politics that they have only one interest. That is to withdraw from the process and let it swirl around them. They are the office ostriches. Suppose you decide that you'd like to withdraw from office politics. Never mind that it can't be done entirely, short of leaving the job. How much can you withdraw, for how long, and at what cost? What's to be protected or gained by that decision, and why are you making it? Are you leaving any paths open for renewing participation down the road?

There is no risk-free decision, just as there is no risk-free working environment. Our research indicates that this is the single, universal mistake people make in office politics. They see no risk in the status quo—in doing nothing. If you analyze it carefully, however, you'll see that this is the highest level of risk most of us assume. Here's why. From the moment you realize that you have a decision to make, you begin, if only subconsciously, to assess the risks of each possible alternative. At the time you first look for alternatives, the greatest number of alternatives is available to you. This is true because you have the most lead time and therefore the most time to adjust, negotiate, or generate alternatives. Look at figure 3. Assume that you are at decision point number 1. Instead of making a choice at this point, you decide to wait for more information, a change in circumstances, or simply a more favorable time, however you may define that. One of the choices, until you reach the fifth decision point, is always to wait until the next decision point. Time passes.

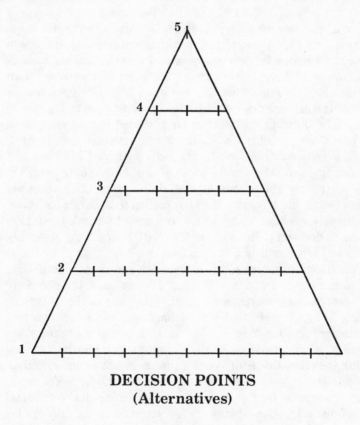

DECISION POINTS
(Alternatives)

Fig. 3

You suddenly remember that you have a decision to make down the road or someone reminds you of that decision. That is decision point number two. If you think about it, you will realize that there are fewer alternatives now, simply because some have been eliminated or rendered unsuitable by the passage of time. You still really don't want to decide, so you put your decision off. The process continues through several more points until one of two things happens: Either the decision no longer needs to be made because the problem has been resolved in some other fashion, or you are faced with a decision that you must accept but that is not really yours. Someone else has made it for you.

By not assessing the risks of the alternatives and making a choice at an early decision point, you face an either/or situation. You either accept the decision in which you had no part or you move on. Chance for risk analysis and negotiation has passed.

As an example of this situation, let's consider a young man named Dan. He knew that his boss's job would be open within six months because the boss was being transferred to the Texas plant. The opening meant that Dan needed to campaign with the boss's boss, a difficult man. It wasn't particularly pleasant to do this. Dan was both well qualified to succeed his boss and anxious to do so. Myopically enough, Dan looked over his peers and, seeing no likely competitors, did nothing. Not until six weeks before his boss left did Dan realize that Sarah had been assiduously working on both the boss and the boss's boss. Dan awoke at decision point number four with his chances of getting the boss's job seriously compromised.

This inaction occurs most often when people are faced with difficult, but not pressing, decisions. For instance, the company may reorganize your department at some time in the future. In fact, it's fairly certain that your department will be reorganized within six months. You would like to see that reorganization increase, not decrease, your department's size and importance within the company. Still, reorganization is just a rumor, and no one has put any specifics into the internal network. You wait. After seven months, top management announces its reorganization plans. While these plans are not set in concrete, they are far more solid than they were when you first realized that a decision was pending. Your choices now are either to accept the decision and try to tinker with the details or to reject it and confront top management with a very high risk to your job and career.

In his excellent book *A Guide to Personal Risk Taking* (New York: American Management Association, 1974), Richard E. Byrd talks about the rules for risk taking. He says that these are: (1) never risk more than you can afford to lose; (2) don't risk a lot for a little; and (3) consider the odds, and then use your intuition. Although he applies his rules to a different set of risks, they fit very well into any analysis of political risk.

The number of people who risk more than they can afford to lose in political warfare is legion. The reason is an inadequate assessment of the risks or no assessment at all. For instance, Jack works for a sales manager who has the temperament and style of the late General George S. Patton. Jack is a good performer, but his boss constantly tries to spur him on with criticism rather than encouragement. One day Jack has had all he can take. He is fed up. Instead of confronting his boss directly, he goes to his boss's boss, the vice-president of sales and marketing, and unloads all his grievances—real and invented. In theory, the vice-president should be sympathetic to Jack. After all, Jack has some legitimate complaints.

But Jack has violated a very important folkway of business. He has broken the chain of command. Furthermore, he has criticized his boss's boss's taste. Jack's boss is a reflection of his boss's taste. Had Jack thought through the possible consequences of his actions, he probably would not have breached the chain of command and gone to his boss's boss. However, in his righteous wrath, he acted without thinking—much less assessing the possible risks. The problem is that he has risked more than he can afford to lose because he's put his job on the line without any other job lined up in case something happens. He has ignored what he knows to be his boss's nature and temperament. He has invited, at best, consignment to the office political deep freeze and, at worst, firing.

Can his boss fire Jack for having gone over his head? The boss probably would not call Jack's behavior insubordination, but if he decided to get rid of Jack, he could certainly find a way— regardless of Jack's performance, past service to the company, or seniority. The problem with assessing how much people have to lose in any risk analysis is that, like Jack, most people undervalue the consequences to the degree that they perceive their own position to be fair, morally right, or just.

Being right in a moral or ethical sense rarely coincides with the right the company sees. The single exception is overt dishonesty. If Jack's immediate boss had had his hand in the till and Jack had blown the whistle on him, Jack would have been in a much stronger position. The boss's boss, much as he might have liked to ignore the situation, would not have dared to do so if Jack could prove his charges or provide strong reason to suspect the boss of fiscal impropriety.

You risk the most politically—almost always more than you can afford to lose—when you question a superior's judgment in a way that puts that person on the defensive. The risks are smallest when you have at your command facts that cast the person's actions in an illegal or questionable light.

When we examine the political validity of Byrd's second rule—don't risk a lot for a little—we can remember one Richard Nixon covering up the burglary of the Democratic national headquarters in the Watergate apartment complex in 1972. The risks of discovery on his part in that caper were the acting out of Byrd's rule. Even if Nixon had discovered that the Democratic party was planning the violent overthrow of the Republican party, it was a big risk. Nothing short of the Democrats' planning a violent political revolution for the whole country could have justified so high a risk. We sophisticated citizens, while scorning Nixon's utter lack of regard for the risks of such a decision, may perhaps do the very same thing in our own careers. For instance, we will risk losing a promotion by violating the boss's or the organization's values simply for the satisfaction of bucking the system. There's certainly nothing wrong with doing that if you have toted up the risks and decided that they are worth it. The problem is that most people don't think that far ahead.

Kate, for example, works for a man who harbors the notion that a woman's place is in the secretarial pool. She has worked five years for the company, and every one of her performance appraisals has been good. One day she learns that a new man has been hired by her boss to fill a position one level above hers, for which she herself had been considered. Before she has had time to marshal her information sources and find out if her background and experience are really roughly comparable with those of the newly hired person's, she puts the word into the grapevine that she is thinking of suing for sex discrimination when the formal announcement is made. Two days later her boss suggests she apply for a transfer or seek a new job.

Kate has risked a great deal for very little. Had she waited and learned more about the new man—even waited until he came aboard so she could interview him personally—her case would have been stronger. The fact that she didn't and that she threatened the boss (even though this threat went through the informal network) drew a strong negative response immediately. She might still be able to sue but only if she can prove her case—an unknown at this time. She was lucky not to be fired outright. She's made it a thousand times more difficult for herself politically within the company and outside when she looks for a new job. Imagine her references!

The issue is not her right to sue. That's indisputable if she has a case. The issue is whether or not she assessed the risks in approaching the problem as she did. Had she said, "I don't care if this costs me my job. It's a matter of principle," nobody would have argued with her. She would have assessed the risks and decided they were not greater than the worth of the issue. Instead, she did not anticipate the probable risk in putting information into the grapevine. She was not prepared, in retrospect, to have risked so much for so little.

People have ways of blocking their own gut reactions to risk. For instance, once you've thought through your options in any situation, you should have some innate feeling about the option that you've determined has the least risk and the greatest possibility of success. Byrd's final rule for risk taking—Consider the odds, and then use your intuition—is especially important in office politics.

Intuition and Ethics

Keep your intuition at the fore instead of blocking it. It will help you quell rash action in favor of more thought and preparation. Intuition is not saying, "What the hell—I'll try it." That's just another kind of brinksmanship. Intuition is actually all your past experiences screened through your subconscious. That filtering process helps you decide what is most important and gives you a sense of what you are most comfortable with. For example, David's boss had been having an affair with a woman who worked for a competitor. Since the boss was married and didn't want his affair publicized, he tried to keep the office from finding out—something almost impossible to pull off. Once a week the boss and his paramour met at her apartment for lunch and fun. David knew the woman, but his boss did not know this.

One day, when the boss was engaged in his extracurricular activity, the local hospital called and said that the boss's oldest son had been admitted as a result of a bicycle accident. The boss was expected back in forty-five minutes, but his son was in critical condition. David's problem was whether to call the woman's apartment or to wait until the boss returned, not letting on that he knew where and with whom the boss was engaged.

This dilemma is faced regularly by many people because they see great risks in knowing something they are not supposed to know. In looking at the odds in this case, however, it's a matter of weighing the likelihood that the child will die, and then the consequences for David in terms of his own conscience, against the odds that the child will live. It's a classic case that we use in our seminars on office politics because it points up the absolute need for people to be ethical on their own terms.

David will have to analyze his decision to call the boss on the basis of two criteria: (1) What are the probable consequences to his career if he does or does not call? and (2) What are the risks of his regretting on a long-term basis that he didn't call if the child dies?

Since David cannot know exactly how serious the child's condition is, his decision is ethical as well as political. No one can tell anyone what to do in this situation—only how to assess the risks. The pain avoiders among us will call. The people with strong ethics will call. People who don't have a clear picture of the boss's temperament and predictability probably will debate long enough for the boss to return, thereby obviating the need for a decision. David called. The boss was glad he did. The child, it turned out, was more scratched up than anything else but had hit his head when he was knocked off the bike. That's why the accident had seemed more serious at first.

Most decisions that are important enough to subject to risk analysis are also important enough to cause a lot of pain and anxiety. The use of risk analysis should reduce some of the pain because it makes the alternatives concrete rather than just "thoughts" swimming around in our brains. The anxiety comes from uncertainty as to both the options and the outcome. No one can live a politically risk-free life as long as he or she continues to work with others.

If you look at the discussion of risk so far, you'll be struck that all of our examples in rules for risk taking are of people who were looking at static risk, that is, "How can I keep what I have?" or "How can I prevent my position from being damaged?" In the next chapter we shall begin using the rules of risk taking for strategy planning. These, of course, are the dynamic risks—risks taken in order to gain something or to influence a decision that will give us something.

As a practice on risk analysis, consider the following example and see how you would assess the risks. Keep in mind that every risk analysis is done from an imperfect knowledge base. You will never have all the information you need. You will always make decisions on the basis of whatever information you have at any one time.

Dick's superior was fired for a performance so indifferent and inept that other inept people were coming around to take notes. After a three-month search, the company triumphantly announced that a hotshot from a competitor had been brought in to head the division. Dick had heard about this woman, Valerie, from friends who worked in the division that Valerie formerly headed. Valerie was in danger of being fired when Dick's company began courting her. In fact, Val's superiors were stunned when Dick's company made her an offer. Top management is firmly behind Valerie, however, and Dick has two options. He can train Valerie thoroughly in her new job (management has assigned this task to him), or he can give her just enough training so that she will fall flat.

Dick's peers and subordinates are about equally divided on whether Valerie should be given a chance to succeed or should be unobtrusively knifed at the water cooler. Both sides see Dick as an ally. Val wants his support. Dick has been with the company long enough to know that there are ways to set Valerie up for failure that could never be traced back to him.

In looking at the risks, Dick will have to assess how likely it is that Valerie will fail. Valerie's problem with her former job may have been political, and she may be dying to throw herself into this new job and make a success of it. Dick will have to assess how much Valerie has been briefed by top management. Does she know that Dick was bypassed for her job and that he would have liked it? Has top management heard any of the rumors about her former job?

For Dick the issues are also ethical ones. How much is he willing to do to skunk Valerie? What's in it for him if he does? Is the pressure from his peers very important? Are there any other options open to him besides the obvious ones?

In the end, Dick will not be able to separate his own ethical concerns from his career problems. If he decides that Valerie must be taught and that it will enhance his own career to do so, he risks her learning the job and consolidating her own power. He may be blocked. If he doesn't teach her the job, top management may blame him, not her.

Whatever Dick decides, he will be better off in terms of risk if he decides quickly. As we discussed, at the first decision point he will have more options and more opportunity to change if something comes up that he hasn't anticipated.

Most people see office politics as entirely amoral. The process is amoral but not the people involved. They have some moral values, however convoluted these values might appear to the casual observer.

When you are looking at risk issues, never try to divorce your own ethics from the situation. To do so leaves you vulnerable. Most of the people who have run afoul of office politics and been most uncomfortable have been people who compromised their own ethics. They were doing things that violated their innate sense of right and wrong. To be vulnerable is to invite others to work against you. People can sense when someone is ethically overextended. You begin to question and agonize over decisions that ordinarily would not bother you. We have seen dozens of people who did not believe in what they were trying to do. Backstabbing and backbiting were not for them. Their participation in office politics should have been limited by their gut responses to what was going on around them.

Instead of saying, as many people do, that office politics is rough and that you have to be able to take it, it would be better to find a less hostile or compromising work environment. If all those around you hold different values and see risks differently, you will always be at a competitive disadvantage. You and your work will suffer. The very nature and content of the work will probably reflect values opposed to your own. The group cannot and will not change to accommodate you. Therefore, once you have determined that you are at odds with your environment, you will have to change the environment—move on.

Suppose, however, that you are not really at odds with your environment but simply an inexperienced participant in need of the rules, just as Elizabeth and Harry were. In that case, you will need to do some strategy planning and set your strategies in motion. That's what chapter 4 is all about.

Chapter 4

Strategy Planning— *or* Machiavelli Was Right

Many people think there's something faintly wicked about strategy planning, as if one were going to scheme to take over the company, dump a boss who displeases one, or stab a colleague with whom one disagrees. Actually, strategy planning is nothing more than developing a plan for moving from point A, where you are now, to point B, where you want to be. Practically every activity involves strategy planning—from the quickest route to the supermarket to rising to the top of AT&T.

PLANNING THE STRATEGY

In the last chapter, we talked about the pillars on which any plan must rest: goals and objectives and risk assessment. Without a knowledge of these key elements, strategy planning is strategy guessing.

Strategy planning always starts with a question of where you want to go. As you look over your career plan, you will see a long-term political goal or goals and short-term objectives. What long-term political goals do you have? How is your participation in office politics going to advance your career in the long run?

Let's suppose that your long-term goal is to be the acknowledged leader in your industry. This is broad enough to keep you motivated and narrow enough to keep you headed in the right direction. Your objectives include being president of your present company or a company of comparable size and stature in the industry. Having said this much, you still have no plan for structuring your participation in your company's internal politics to help you do this. You are still in the passive position of no win, no lose. In order to understand what office politics can do for you, you first have to decide what you want.

We've talked about the importance of assessing the hierarchy and competition (temperature chart) and the need to control the internal information network, tapping into it at as many different sources as possible. We've talked about distancing yourself emotionally from the pain of office push and shove. The time has come to plan some active intervention in the political life of the office.

The first step is to cement good working relationships with everybody. If you did not accomplish this after reading the network-building section, do it now. This seems elementary until you think about the people in your work environment you'd really like to see take a fall. You'll have to submerge those thoughts, or you'll be a handicapped player. There's no sense trying to plan strategy predicated on revenge unless revenge is going to advance your career. Even Machiavelli, the ultimate political strategist, saw revenge as a limited tool and motivator.

By good working relationships we mean amiable enough to allow you to trade information, to hold the respect of others, and to be able to cooperate with minimal jealousy and obstruction. You'll know that you have good working relationships when people look to you for the same things. Reciprocity is the key.

After you're sure that you have good working relationships with your superiors, subordinates, and, most importantly, your peers, it is time to decide on some specific short-term objectives. Here are some questions that may aid you in generating your own objectives.

1. Whom would you like to get to know better for any of the following reasons:

    a. The person has great power and influence and could help your career directly.

   b. The person has specific knowledge that you need.

   c. The person has contacts within the company—or within the industry that you would like to tap into.

   d. The person could give you some insight into how he or she got to his or her present position.

2. Are there any job openings or promotions that you'd like immediately? Does the opening or promotion fit in with your long-range goals?

3. Your current boss is about to be replaced, and there is uncertainty about his or her replacement and that person's values, management style, and power within the organization. What will this change mean for you?

4. Your boss does not like you and has made this clear. You are in danger of being either fired or bypassed for another person more to the boss's liking. At this moment and in this situation you are nonpromotable. Would making a change be worthwhile? If you stay, what do you need to do to improve the situation?

5. You are at odds with the values of the people and the organization, and it's just a matter of time until you are either fired or leave in disgust. Where should you go, and how should you go about finding that place?

These questions fall roughly into three groups: (1) those whose objective is to get someone else to do something for you (questions 1 and 2); (2) those whose objective is to keep someone else from doing something to you (questions 3 and 4); and (3) those whose objective is to keep others from stopping you from doing something that you want to do (question 5). You can do nothing without some cooperation from others.

Thus there are three kinds of behaviors we want from people. We want them to help us when we need their help, not hurt us at any time, and not get in the way when we're trying to do something for ourselves.

Obviously we'll never get complete control over other people's behavior. That's why talking about managing or controlling people is somewhat useless. Our major tools will always be persuasion and negotiation.

Still, we can do more than we're doing now if we have objectives and a plan. For instance, if we want to prevent the boss

from doing something—it isn't necessary for him or her to realize our intention—we may plan to lead the boss to not doing it
in one of three ways. We may succeed simply by not making a
big fuss over the issue, by ignoring it entirely, or by making the
issue seem very trivial.

For example, Ken always had to put out reports in his boss's
name. With each report, his blood pressure rose ten points because he thought it unfair that he received no credit for his
work. One day at a conference with his boss's boss, Ken found
himself answering all the questions that came up—many of
which his boss was unable even to grasp. The result, over time,
was that Ken's self-esteem and position within the organization
rose. His boss could not stop that process because he could not
fill the information gap. Had Ken confronted his boss demanding recognition, he'd have turned the boss into an enemy. Ken
would also have shown others his lack of respect for the power
structure.

Office politics requires some leadership qualities. You have to
be able to lead people to do or not do whatever you want done or
left undone. People call this manipulation if they dislike it, leadership if they admire it. The difference is purely semantic. Manipulation is nothing more or less than leadership. Leadership,
imbued with heroic overtones as it is, is nothing more or less
than getting people, by whatever means, to follow.

Therefore we are not going to talk about manipulating but
about leading and influencing people in whatever direction we
want them to go. To talk otherwise implies that people are
sheep without the capacity to reach a decision on their own. You
have to have worked in an office undergoing major reorganization to appreciate how quickly even the most sheeplike employees can turn into tigers.

After thinking through your own situation, it may occur to
you that one thing that would advance your career and you
politically would be to have more contact with your boss's boss.
That way when your boss is promoted or moves on, you'll be
heir apparent to the boss's job. You realize that this sort of
thinking might cause the boss to break out in paranoia. Whatever you attempt should look like an accident or at least not
appear to be part of a grand and Machiavellian strategy.

So you start to develop a strategy to bring yourself into closer contact with Fred, your boss's boss, without endangering your relationship with your own boss, Ellen. Your objective in developing this closer contact is two-fold: (1) If your boss moves on within the organization or even outside, you'd be in line for her job; and (2) there is a great deal you can learn about the business from Fred, and some of it would help you in long-range career planning. With the information Fred can give you, you can choose an appropriate long-range goal because you will be aware of more of the possibilities.

The first step in your plan is to go back to your temperature chart and review the data you've collected on both Ellen and Fred. You note that Fred went to the same school your father attended. This is a plus, as the school has a fine basketball team and many devoted alumni. It will certainly serve as an opening conversational gambit.

Fred also belongs to the industry's leading trade organization. Membership in that organization would be a worthwhile investment. Just attending the meetings could be worthwhile even if you don't join, as it would bring you and Fred into informal but legitimate contact. It might also provide information needed to broaden your present knowledge of your job, profession, organization, and industry. It could bring you to the attention of other influential people.

Your informal network suggests that Fred is interested in sports and plays racquetball. You may also play racquetball or at least would be willing to learn.

Your immediate plan is to establish a friendlier relationship with Fred without arousing the suspicions of Ellen. You've developed a few alternatives that you might employ in increasing your contacts with Fred. It's now time to evaluate the risks of implementing any or all of these.

The fact that you are not after Ellen's job right now, though you may be in a few years, is not going to mean much if Ellen thinks you are and acts on that assumption. Therefore, your risk assessment starts with her. She is in the best position to harm you. Of your three strategies—seeking more contact with Fred informally at the office by talking about his alma mater, meeting him at trade association meetings, or trying to get into his racquetball league—which would have the least risk of damaging your relationship with Ellen?

You refer to your temperature chart and decide that while the first is most direct, it's also most risky and requires the highest level of social skill. The second presents the least problems, but will take the longest time, since Fred may not attend every association meeting and you may miss them occasionally as well. The third alternative is probably less risky than the first alternative, but it requires the most assertiveness.

In order to join Fred's racquetball group, you're going to have to be at about Fred's level of skill. Then, too, someone is probably going to have to bring you into the group. It would be fairly high risk to approach Fred and ask him to play unless you have been playing regularly with others from the organization. This will take some time to set up. If you are female, it will be doubly difficult because, unless there are other women, you will have to be an excellent racquetball player to be included in the group. The hours of practice required to develop your skill might be more profitably spent on some other aspect of your career.

As you look at the alternatives, you'll want to put them in order from the easiest to do to the most difficult. What is the probability of success with each alternative? After you've done this, ask yourself which of the alternatives looks best overall. As you're doing this, you may come up with some other ideas as well. Subject these newcomers to the same analysis, and give each its rightful place on your priority list. You're now ready to name one of these alternatives Plan I.

Plan I should be the plan that you see as the least risky with the highest probability of success. At the same time, you should decide on your backup strategy, or Plan II. Every strategy needs an alternative in case Plan I doesn't work. You don't want to have to return to square one just because of one thing you couldn't, or didn't, foresee.

Before you take any action, there is one thing you must do: Give your Plan I a time frame. How long will you use that plan before you decide it's not going to work? Can you commit three months? six months? a year? You must give yourself a time frame and be prepared to reevaluate your plan at the end of the time you've allotted.

Many, many people who might otherwise qualify as good strategists simply refuse to hem themselves in with a specific time limit. This is the opposite of effective strategy planning. In leaving the time open-ended, you lock out any possibility of changing an unsuccessful strategy or altering it to make it more successful if the need arises. Open-ended strategies are not strategies at all—just wishful thinking.

After you have set a reasonable time limit, divide it into thirds. That is, if you have allotted six months for yourself and Fred to get on a friendlier basis, divide six months into three two-month periods. These are your checkpoints. There is no sense in waiting six months before you begin a careful evaluation of how things are going. You need to evaluate at regular intervals. The plan should first be reviewed a third of the way through. Otherwise you will not have enough time to adjust it.

The first checkpoint is especially crucial because it's early enough to make major adjustments if you got off to a poor start. Two thirds of the way through you should have an excellent sense of whether your strategy is working. If it's not, there's still enough time to make adjustments. You will also know whether you need more time to reach your objective and can adjust your time frame accordingly.

Begin monitoring your plan as soon as you put it into motion. Once you begin a particular course of action, you should feel some commitment to carrying it through. If you are working on Fred, it would be awkward not to continue to build that relationship, at least until it stabilizes. Sudden changes in any relationship always create suspicion, resentment, and hostility. Fred may notice he's been dropped. If so, you will have created a negative relationship. If Fred is not immediately responsive to your overtures, there's no reason to give up and look for an alternative plan with different people. Office politics is the building of human relationships and the apportioning of power. Both processes take time. What you can do, however, is monitor carefully whether progress is being made toward your ultimate goal and how your actions affect other objectives.

EVALUATING THE RESULTS

After you've achieved your objective, or realized that there is no hope of achieving it, you must evaluate. How did things go? How accurate were your predictions? Would you use the same strategy again? You don't necessarily have to write this down, but you must talk consciously to yourself about your results. If you don't do this, you'll forget what you've learned. You'll be just like the man who went to Colorado for a three-week vacation. He did not make any particular note of the many beautiful things he saw. All he said to himself was that he was having "a swell time." A year and a half later the man's total recall of his vacation was that he'd had "a swell time." Not very helpful in planning a vacation or a career.

The problems in evaluating political strategies are the same as those in evaluating the effects of advertising. It is as difficult to say that one particular advertisement caused one person to buy a car as it would be to say that one particular conversation caused your boss to promote you. The effect is cumulative rather than one specific action producing, or equaling, a direct result.

A second problem with evaluating the results is that you may have underestimated the time it takes to develop sufficient rapport, build support systems and information networks, or convince someone by gentle persuasion to do something for you. Unlike government elections, there is no one day on which votes must be cast and counted. You cannot command a vote on an issue in the office unless you're dealing with unions. You have to be sensitive to the cues you do receive. And you have to be able to readjust your time frame to the actual scheduling of events in the office.

Third, the process of evaluation is ongoing, as is the entire political process. Even though we will always evaluate at our checkpoints and at what we'll call the "end" of a strategy, we are constantly evaluating each move as we go along. This is necessary because it shows us where we are, how we're doing, and where we should be moving.

One of two things tends to happen in political evaluations. Either we misinterpret the results because what we've done produced a result different from what we expected, or we see no change. As a society we expect change to be as large as the political changes we see at election time. Office political changes tend to be very small and generally involve attitudes or behaviors of individuals rather than groups.

Persuasion means changing attitudes and then behaviors. Forceable change tends to concentrate on changing behaviors without changing attitudes. This is the method of many affirmative action programs. Obviously there's a need for the change of behaviors and then attitudes, but office politics is more concerned with first changing attitudes and then behaviors. That's because it's less disruptive to go at attitudes first. It also takes much more raw power to change behaviors. People will get used to an idea and adapt their behavior accordingly.

This means that a lot of the measurement of results in office politics will depend on measuring changes in attitude through the informal network. Do not expect more than an inference of change. That is, if you want to know whether your boss sees you in a more favorable light, don't expect that you'll hear that he does in exactly those words. If he mentions your name more often in a positive way, this is a clue, and you could infer that the relationship is improving. Likewise, if you can find no clue that the boss talks about you at all, depending on the nature of the boss, you can probably infer that he or she has not warmed to you and that you need to work on the relationship.

If you hear nothing while you're trying to evaluate your efforts, the worst thing you can do is change your strategy. Change should always be a last resort, and then only after you've made a careful evaluation. Otherwise you will be unable to evaluate any of your strategies because they will become jumbled together. The cumulative effort will be tangled, and anything you might learn might be too woven together to separate from the rest.

Given that situation, how do you evaluate your strategies once you have put them into effect? The five possible outcomes of strategy planning and the ways to measure them in office politics are as follows:

1. *The event you planned to influence comes out your way.*
You campaigned for the promotion and got it. This may be tricky because you might have gotten it without doing anything. If you hadn't campaigned, however, you might not have gotten the promotion. The risk in campaigning for promotion, or in not campaigning, was equally great in hindsight. But hindsight is of little value. At the time you decided to try to influence events, your exact chances of getting the promotion were unknown. Therefore, without some strategy, the outcome would have been left to chance.

2. *The event you sought to prevent did not happen.*

This is known as protective politics or the avoidance of negative factors. If you were campaigning to keep a particularly obnoxious superior or peer from being named manager and the person did not become manager, you may have influenced events. Your influence may have caused others to examine the candidate more closely. You know that you had influence because people are repeating negatives about the candidate that you first put into the informal network. Keep in mind that the informal network tends to carry impressions rather than exact repetition. Therefore, if the network is carrying your phrases or even items on your agenda, it means that you put the information into the proper network. It also means that someone more powerful than you has taken up your cause or point of view. This can be a problem if people discover that the network's phrases came from you. Only you should be able to recognize what you put in. If you are engaged in limiting someone else's career, protective coloring is going to be very important. It is especially important if someone else is likely to go after you if you're found out. Assume that this would happen.

Our research indicates that it makes little difference whether the information you circulate that damages someone's career is true or false. There is a political taboo against hurting other people's careers even with the mere recitation of facts. Many people see this as unsportsmanslike conduct, just as they dislike reading bad news in newspapers or seeing it on television. You have to be careful.

3. *Information you put into the network has come back to you attributed to a powerful person.*

You are the only one who had access to a particular set of facts. You put that information into the network. Someone more powerful takes up the cause or is seen as owning the idea or information rather than you. This can help you identify your potential allies.

4. *The network increases your visibility.*

If your campaign was one of building greater visibility for yourself, you can measure the results by keeping track of the number of people you did not know before your campaign who now seek you out. The natural tendency is for those who have the most power to seek out those who are supposed to be getting more power. This is known as "eyeballing the competition."

5. *You did not get what you wanted—a promotion—but you got something, even though it was just an explanation.*

The more those above you feel the need to explain what they're doing, the more successful your strategy. One promotion is not nearly as important as an ongoing dialogue with your superiors. That's the only way you'll find out whether they have better things in mind for you or whether you're dead-ended. They may feel you are a good worker where you are. They'll do anything to keep you content except promote you.

Assume that the more you interact with people at your level and in the levels above you, the more likely you are to be able to use the network to get the kind of information you need. This information-gathering process is crucial to any kind of political activity. If you thoroughly understand the process, you can get results.

We talked about checkpoints and the value of using them to measure how you're doing while there's still time to make changes. One of the problems every office politician faces is the need to act quickly as conditions change. This is where most people go awry. They don't know when to adapt their strategies to new or unexpected situations. If you don't have a finger on the pulse almost all the time, you won't know when you need to change strategies or when panic may be the correct response.

Let's look at an actual case. Say you want a promotion and you know an opening exists. Your plan has been to raise your visibility with your boss and your boss's boss. You have let both know that you want that promotion. Your network feeds back to you that Joe is the front-runner but that no final decision will be made for one week.

You are at checkpoint 1 in your timetable because you'd planned on a three-month campaign for the job. Your network sources hadn't reported that the job was to be filled so quickly. So far your strategy has worked. Both your boss and your boss's boss are aware that you are interested and seem to think of you as productive and potentially promotable. Still, unless you do something more active, Joe appears to be the choice. You are aware, of course, that even if you increase your activity, you may still not get the promotion. Joe may be in so solidly for the job that nothing could make a difference. That is unknowable right now.

At this point you go through the process outlined earlier in the chapter. You weigh alternatives and pick your Plan I and Plan II. You consider what will help you reach your new objective—getting the promotion—within the one-week time frame.

You choose a new strategy. You'll seriously discuss your future with your boss and let the boss's boss hear through his network that you're really concerned about your advancement potential within the company. Many people hesitate to let their superiors know how strongly they feel about this sort of thing. These timid ones fear someone will feel threatened. Letting people know you're concerned is not the same as threatening to leave when and if you don't get what you want. Only a *threat* is a threat.

There is the possibility that your strategy won't work, but it has two things going for it. First, it's direct. This is not the time to hint. Ask for what you want. Second, you're acting on two fronts. If you concentrate on your boss alone, you risk his or her being swayed by his or her boss, whom you haven't even tried to influence. All strategy changes must have these two elements: They must be direct and they must work on more than one power source. This is the only way you can hope to telescope the time frame enough to get what you want.

Your strategy plan should include an alternative of choices for your boss when you talk with him or her. If you ask for the promotion, the answer can be either yes or no. What you want is for the answer to be either the promotion or something else, not the promotion or nothing. For instance, if you ask for a promotion *or* job restructuring along specific lines, you'll have a much better chance of some kind of compromise that moves you forward. This is an old selling technique. Ask the customers not whether they want the product, yes or no, but whether they'd like five or ten gross. They'll have to work to say no.

So far we've walked through strategy planning at the simplest level. Now we have some good news and some bad news. The good news is that whether you're working on six plans involving many people or on one plan with one person, the process is the same. It is the same process from goal setting to evaluation. The bad news is that most of us are juggling many plans at the same time and therefore face a higher risk of problems in remembering where we are in any particular plan and why. This is the strategist's occupational hazard. That is why, if you are to succeed in office politics, you'll have to write down your plans, time frames, and checkpoints. Without written records you'll have a very difficult time doing more than one thing at a time.

Two concerns haunt strategy planners. These are (1) How do I know whether what I'm planning is realistic? and (2) How can I predict the probability of my doing successfully whatever I'm trying to do?

If there were specific, never-fail formulas for dealing with either reality testing or success predictions, we'd have many more converts to strategy planning.

Reality testing is the bugaboo of the beginning worker and of the person with poor skills in reading other people's reactions. If you think you have devised a great plan but want a reading on the reality of the strategy, go to your network in either your own company or another one and try to find out if anyone has ever done anything similar. For example, if you'd like your job restructured along particular lines, it's important to check to see if any company like yours has a similar job. This can also be a selling point. If, without revealing specifics, you can get some feedback on your strategy, so much the better. If you have any doubts that what you plan is possible, consult someone who's had more work experience. Above all, don't plunge in. Remember, if you are a neophyte, it's not good to start with something involving several strategies and more than one or two people. Start small until you've had a chance to practice the process. It takes time and experience to learn how to do this well.

MINIMIZING RISK

If you are in a high-risk situation—it would be possible to lose your job if your strategy failed, for instance—try your strategies in a volunteer setting or in a trade association before you put your job on the line. If things are shaky and you don't have an alternative lined up, you must first protect your paycheck. This is not the time to be heroic.

Trite and tacky as it sounds, a good rule for office politics really is the golden rule. It doesn't work all of the time. Plenty of people are going to do things to you that they certainly wouldn't want anyone to do to them. You will still have to adjust your strategies to fit your ethics. Do not do anything or plan to do anything that you know at gut level would make you uncomfortable or that violates your personal ethics. You will make mistakes, alienate people—even create unnecessary enemies—if you begin doing things you can't live with ethically.

If you see yourself behaving unethically, it is certain to give your ego the shakes. This has nothing to do with morality as defined by any particular group but morality as you see it. Acting in a way you believe to be fundamentally wrong makes you insecure in yourself and your actions across the board, whether they apply to the unethical strategy or not.

The best-laid plans don't always work out—in spite of meticulous planning, careful execution, and attention to detail. Indeed, in office politics, as in life, there is no guarantee that while you're developing a strategy someone else isn't developing a counterstrategy to reach the same objective. In a dynamic situation, which any office is, it's almost assured. This proves that it is necessary to act in defensive ways, too.

Most people, if they're honest with themselves, are pain avoiders. If they don't know that someone else is trying to beat them out of a job or promotion, or is just enmeshed in a power scramble, they will plan, execute, and evaluate in fine fashion. As soon as Jan learns that she has head-to-head competition, pain avoidance will come into play. Jan will do one of a number of things depending on her belief in the original plan and her degree of desire to reach her goal. She may give up the plan and withdraw from the battle. She may intensify her efforts. She may change some tactics.

Until now, Jan didn't know that there was a battle. She thought she alone was campaigning. Because there is competition and the danger that Jan might be beaten by someone else, rather than failing on her own, Jan may decide to avoid the pain and give up the contest.

You can see that Jan didn't think it was a contest until she knew there was a competitor. One of the problems of office politics is that people forget that there will always be competition. You will never have the field to yourself. You will always try to increase your share of a scarce commodity, power, at someone else's expense. If you find this distasteful, you will be a defensive player only. But as we've said before, you will never be able to opt out of the process entirely.

Avoiding competition on the theory that it is less painful if avoided is not a very successful strategy. It simply can't be done. Others are going to be stepping on you or your turf whether you invite them to or not. You cannot be self-effacing enough to go unnoticed as long as you're on the payroll because too many people will use the situation to their advantage to take credit for your ideas and actions. If you don't defend and promote yourself, no one else will. There is no more self-defeating strategy than waiting for recognition.

There is no way to avoid some pain in office politics. Personal distancing helps but is no panacea. You can, however, learn from what other people have done and avoid some of the most common political pitfalls.

1. *Don't get involved in a political action unless you have no personal stake or unless there is not some short-term or long-term advantage to you or your career.*

If Jeff is being abused by the boss, offer him your help and advice privately. Turning Jeff into a "cause" will alienate the boss, cast you as the office reformer, and cause other people to seek your help and protection. To what end? If you can't fit this role into your own long-term career goals, you're wasting energy. You will spend all your time on other people's problems, and you probably won't help Jeff. Why put your own job on the line for anything other than your own interest? The exception: If you feel so strongly at an ethical level about the problems that you must act, then act, but limit your action to the specific problem—not general reform.

We are not saying don't care but rather don't sacrifice your own position in a way that will help neither you nor the victims. And don't unsheathe your sword until you've checked the facts and assessed the risks. This may seem elementary, but how many times have you said—and heard your peers say—that something's not fair! The belief that business, government, or nonprofit organizations must treat employees fairly stands right up there with the old saw that everybody should love everybody else. It won't happen. Your goal in becoming politically streetwise is to pick your battles, not be picked by them. You can't

reform the organization unless you are rather high up on the
chart. There's significant doubt that *anyone* gets that high. Any
strategy that asks you to exercise more power than you have
invites failure.

Jumping in against your boss to save a peer means trying to
exercise more power than you have. It is only logical that your
boss can command more power than you can. If you are in a
power struggle with him or her over a third party, you will probably lose unless you get help from a powerful ally. Bringing in
allies complicates the process and widens the war. You also lose
a great deal of control over your own actions if you have others
to consider. Generals in any kind of battle have logistical problems. Bluntly stated, there are too many problems in fighting
other people's wars. Fight your own unless there are ethical considerations that you can't ignore.

2. *Don't set some event in motion and then, unexpectedly, try
to change direction in order to save face.*

First, in office politics events tend to blend together in a flow
rather than bump along as a series of short, discrete events.
People have general, rather than specific, impressions. It's rarely
possible to take back a rumor or a trial balloon or to reverse an
impression you've spent considerable time and energy building
up. If you've spent a lot of time over several months building an
image as a hard charger seeking challenge and promotion, you'll
have a hard time convincing people that you're not disappointed, so why not acknowledge it? Any other behavior casts
you as either inconsistent or a hypocrite—neither a particularly
flattering image. You might as well be honest—it's the smart
thing politically.

"Letting it all hang out" or "being perfectly frank" is the
worst strategy you can adopt. People mistake honesty for candor. Honesty means that what you say has a factual base and
can be verified. Candor means telling all—neither discretion nor
diplomacy. Candor is poor strategy in office politics because your
verbal shots from the hip may trip you up down the road. You
don't want to lock yourself in unless you are certain that what
you've locked yourself into is what you'll want three or even six
months from now—or tomorrow.

Even though you may discuss your strategy for getting a promotion with a noncompetitive peer, you will not want to discuss

specifics. Confidences can be breached because of the other person's perceived interests. Don't risk your career with that kind of careless confidence. Floating a trial balloon is vastly different from laying out the specifics of your ideas, plans, and methods. Don't do the latter unless you want imitators and aroused competitors. You don't have to tell lies, but you don't have to tell secrets either. Sometimes silence is best.

3. *Building close friendships with peers who are head-to-head competitors is a fatal error.*

You can't expect your friends to provide the kind of support any person needs during battle if those friends' interests are identical with yours and each feels the need to protect himself or herself. Friendships don't thrive on close competition. Better to form loose alliances with peers than turn to them for support that asks them to undercut their own interests. If you think about it, a person not in the thick of battle would make a better friend and provide more comfort than someone who really needs the same kind of support from you at the same time. That sort of burden produces hurt feelings and conflicts of interest.

This is always a hard sell with young workers. They tend to forget the intense grade competition of high school and college. If you remember how you maneuvered to get the A or win the teacher's approval, you remember that your closest competitor was rarely your best friend. The competition kept you apart. The same is true in the office. Trying to impose tight, mutual support and trust on top of intense competition is impossible.

4. *Don't date anyone who works in your office.*

If the person works in another division and there is no way the two of you would ever be working together, fine. Dating, affairs, marriages, and so on are intense, exclusive relationships. Despite your best efforts at secrecy, if you are involved with someone in the office, everybody will know. Don't kid yourself— they have a sixth sense about these things, just as you do.

No one will believe that if you are joined at the hip with Russ or Nancy, you can really treat that person exactly the same as all the other people who are his or her competitors. If the loved one is above or below you on the ladder, it multiplies the problems because you will be seen as either seeking an advantage or giving one. Even if the other person is the love of your life, one of you should change jobs. No one is going to believe that you are capable of the superhuman impartiality required in such a situation.

Sometimes women think that it might be possible to use sex with a boss as the key to the executive suite. When there were fewer opportunities for women, few could have lacked sympathy for the ambitious woman who saw this as the best shot she had. Three things have changed since the sixties. First, affirmative action has frightened a great many companies into offering at least token positions to women. Second, women's views of themselves have changed, and their abilities to compete have sharpened to the point that they no longer see sex as a useful strategy. Third, few men feel they need to barter for sex. Of course, there will always be the dinosaurs who want to trade promotions for sex, just as there will always be call girls and customers. But in the end this strategy results in intense peer dislike and even official organizational disapproval.

5. *Politics does have a certain internal logic under normal conditions.*

If you are doing things in the name of office politics that defy logic and common sense, something is not kosher. You are either misreading the situation or ignoring some vital element. The more successful your strategy, the more likely you will be to arouse enemies who really shouldn't care what you do. Never try to reduce human motives to anything as simple as "People only respond when their ox is being gored." Even nations aren't *that* sensible—remember Vietnam?

Ernie, whose peers and competitors are other men of the same age, is very popular with the women in the office. When he is promoted later, he can expect the combination of personal popularity and political popularity with his boss to result in one or two implacable enemies. That could be predicted and written off to jealousy. Ernie will be surprised, however, when he hears that a particular senior executive in a wholly unrelated department with whom he has no interaction speaks of him as a "no-talent playboy." This kind of indirect criticism tends to unsettle otherwise confident politicians.

It seems almost Kafkaesque that a man two divisions away and two levels up on the chart would be concerned about a middle manager who is not directly competitive nor ever likely to be. Whatever motivates the senior officer to take note of

Ernie's success and treat it negatively can't be worth brooding about. Nothing can be done about it. Some enemies must be accepted and left alone. It may be necessary later to take some action if the enemy starts causing trouble, but to go to the person now on the basis of a rumor would be fatal. Who would not deny the whole thing or respond defensively? Who wouldn't believe that Ernie was crazy to bring it up?

Women often face this problem when, after promotion, their former peers turn into enemies. Charges float around the office that Joyce is high-hatting her former pals. Men and women will tend to use identical terms in describing Joyce. Part of this is jealousy, but part of it is that Joyce herself really is different. Her role is different. If she got her promotion because she worked for it, asked for it, and behaved as if she would fit the new role perfectly, she will be seen as pushy. If she acts surprised—as if she really didn't deserve it—the corporate version of a surprise birthday party—she'd be seen (rightly) as a hypocrite. Either way Joyce is going to have a few enemies who won't really be able to accept her in her new role. That goes with the territory. There is no way that a person can move up in an organization without leaving a bruised soul here and there.

Unfortunately, people tend to assume that only the ambitious have strategies that succeed. Therefore, it is only the ambitious who make enemies. Not so. Pete races sports cars on the weekends. It's the most important part of his life. He works at his job to support his habit. His strategy is to work very hard forty hours per week, assume minimal responsibility, and avoid both overtime and promotions. Pete gets in nobody's way. He should have no enemies because he is not competing with anyone for more power or for a promotion. One day the department head offers Pete a promotion. The atmosphere heats up—charged with menace and much whispering at the office copying machine. The troops are incensed. This is reflected in their obvious hostility toward Pete—not the boss. Doing internal public relations at this point will probably only intensify the anger and shock. A better strategy to diffuse the situation is for Pete to have coffee or lunch or a drink after work with the person he had been friendliest with within the group and try to win that person back. To ignore the hostility in a very small group, regardless of the right or wrong of the situation, will intensify the feeling rather than reduce it. The angry people feel that it's up to Pete to placate them—not up to them to handle their own feelings. After all, he's the cause of their discomfort. This is not only political reality; it's human reality.

The worst thing any person can do in any of these situations is to say, "This isn't fair—these people are not being fair to me," and act accordingly. It's not a question of fairness as much as protecting your own interests. If people feel a particular way, you'll get nowhere in telling them they can't feel that way. The most important thing you must do is divorce your feelings of what's right or fair from the political realities. Do this without being unethical. We trust that you are an ethical person and wouldn't act in unethical or immoral ways. Acting in your own best interest means not giving in to your own feelings while you try to deal with the feelings of others.

IMPROVING YOUR INTERNAL RELATIONSHIPS

All of this brings us to some tips on improving internal relationships overall. You need to promote yourself for these reasons:

1. It helps you get promoted within the organization.

2. If you are known as someone who performs outstandingly well, you will be among the last to get the ax in times of political turmoil.

3. It helps you recruit a mentor (godfather) without whom your assault on the top may be futile. (See chapter 7.)

Here are some ways to promote yourself internally.

1. When you have finished a project or a section of an ongoing assignment, write a memo (one page) to your boss summarizing what has been accomplished. Do this even if you report on this work regularly. Oral reports are worth one-twentieth of written reports. Start by saying, "I know you'll be interested to learn how much we've done . . ."

2. See that the secretaries know that you perform well and what you do. They all stand in well with their bosses.

3. Seek coverage for your work in the local business press or in the business section of the dailies. Your company's top people read that sort of thing. The *Wall Street Journal* is tops, but any newspaper or magazine is useful.

4. Never miss an opportunity to speak before a trade or professional group. The company will see this as a favorable reflection on the organization. Naturally you will let your boss know that you've been asked.

5. Recruit a mentor in your organization. Part of the mentor's function is to help you become more visible.

6. Never turn down any opportunity that will make you more visible in a positive way. Example: Be your department or section's correspondent for the house organ. Even the Crusade of Mercy or United Fund provides good exposure.

7. Use trade shows as a way to reach people in your own organization through the competitors you meet. The word will get back to your company that some of the competitors' people were impressed by you.

All these tools will come in handy as we turn to the problems of workers in situations out of control.

Chapter 5

The Employee as Victim—*or* Is It My Breath?

Elizabeth, our heroine from chapter 1, always felt that she was a particularly rational person. She knew she was intelligent and, before she started working, rarely questioned her own judgments. She was also self-directed and motivated—she knew what she wanted to do with her life. After consulting with a career counselor in college, she developed a career plan using many of the strategies outlined in chapter 4. But when she started working at her new job, something didn't add up.

Elizabeth was most disturbed by the unmistakable feeling that the situation was out of control. As she gradually became aware of the political problems in her office, it seemed to her that everything she said or did caused problems and further alienated her boss. Elizabeth felt as if she were a victim. She was especially disturbed by two things. First, everything she did seemed to be questioned for implications. If she came back from lunch ten minutes early, her boss would ask why. When she handed in a ten-page report, her boss would ask why it was so incomplete or so wordy. Second, her boss kept giving hints to her, and to everybody else, that she was displeased with Elizabeth. This tended to isolate Elizabeth from her fellow workers, who wanted no part of either the impending storm or the guilt by association.

Elizabeth was caught between confronting the boss directly to ask what was wrong and what she had done or failed to do and the idea of appearing paranoid, foolish, or simply young if she did. There was always the chance that the boss would say that Elizabeth was imagining everything.

But Elizabeth wasn't imagining her problems. She was, in fact, a victim. The problem with political victimization is that it defies logic and, therefore, we tend to think we're imagining what's happening and what we feel. Why should Elizabeth's boss want to torture her? Why not just fire her? It was months later, and only on a fluke, that Elizabeth learned that her boss felt threatened by Elizabeth's youth, energy, and ambition. Elizabeth's boss may not have been able to get rid of her rationally, so torture remained the only tool at her disposal. Because such situations seem totally illogical, many people with Elizabeth's problems, including Elizabeth, don't grasp what's going on. That accounts for their dismissing the feeling that they've been victimized, thinking that something is wrong with them, until the victimization has been going on for some time or until it's so obvious that other people have begun to notice.

Elizabeth didn't realize the extent of her problems until she overheard two women she worked with talking in the rest room. One said to the other that she'd been specifically told by the boss "not to let Elizabeth in on anything, as she's not likely to be here much longer." That was when Elizabeth panicked.

Nobody likes being a victim. Most of us want some control over our working lives. The only way to exert any measure of control is early diagnosis. Instead of drowning in your own paranoia, you need to look at the situations that lend themselves most readily to victimization and examine the strategies that are open to you in dealing with them. Keep in mind that anyone who works more than a few years can expect to meet one or more of these situations. Thus, it's worthwhile to be able to read storm clouds before the rain begins.

People become victims in one of three common ways. The first two ways victimize the individual as part of a group solely because he or she is a member of the group. The third victimizes the individual as an individual. That was Elizabeth's problem. These three forms of victimization can be described as follows:

1. Unforeseen and apparently inexplicable change.

2. Mergers, takeovers, acquisitions, and reorganizations.

3. Enemies and scapegoats.

We will examine each of these situations in some detail because, in order to cope with them, you'll need to be able to recognize them early on.

UNFORESEEN CHANGE

Unforeseen change is the most common cause of worker victimization and resultant panic. It involves sudden, unexplained—even inexplicable—change and results in panic up and down the organization.

Regardless of how top and middle management see it, the politics of an organization begins to change immediately in response. As discussed in chapter 1, power relationships are fluid. A change in any of the organization's relationships changes the power relationships and hence the internal politics.

There are three kinds of unforeseen change. It's rare that one kind alone triggers massive change. Usually it's a combination of two of the three. These three are as follows:

1. A key figure in the company is removed because he or she resigned, was fired, or died, and there is no obvious crown prince or princess in the wings ready to take over.

2. The organization loses the energy and direction that it had earlier, appearing to drift or stagnate, and enough people remember how things used to be to be affected by the contrast. Their recognition of the change is sudden and collective.

3. The organization's competitive position changes dramatically and suddenly, though the people in the organization may be slow to recognize it. A product may be made obsolete by a competitor's discovery or by a radical change in population groups. The market may evaporate overnight.

Each one of these situations is forced on all the employees as a group. It changes previously agreeable working relationships and creates a power vacuum. We shall examine each of these kinds of change individually. First, let's look at how all three affect the people involved.

In most cases the change feels like being mugged. It has been quick and irrational and has provoked panic at all levels in the organization. It would have been difficult to predict the change, but the sudden recognition of it is the beginning.

The panic that grips people during one of these events is based on two fears. First, there is the fear of uncontrolled and uncontrollable change, with no heed paid to the status quo. "What will happen to me?" The higher up the ladder, the more this unpredictability unsettles. These are the people with the most to lose. Lost control is important because many people who manage businesses at any level value the power to control what happens to their own work lives and to the lives of those under them.

Imagine the feelings of an army general when something happens and the troops begin running around quite independent of his control. Further, imagine his feelings in this situation if he is unable to give orders and unable to command the troops to act or not to act in a particular way. That is very much the situation of both top and middle management in each of these sudden change situations.

The other fear in a changing situation is really the bottom line throughout the organization—fear of losing one's job. If there is one thing most people fear and dislike intensely, it's job hunting. For a great many people every career move is designed to put off permanently ever having to job hunt. They don't enjoy any part of the process—writing résumés, answering ads, going for interviews. After the realization that changes are afoot, the instant gut reaction is to say, "Oh, God, does this mean I'll be fired or laid off? Will I have to look for a new job?" Far more than losing the paycheck, most people loathe having to go through the entire wearisome, frightening, disorienting process of finding a new job. At this point keeping the job is the only concern.

Once the nature of the event that has caused this change in the organization's life and direction is better understood, principle may come into play. Until people have some idea of what's happening and why, they are striking out irrationally, desperately trying to protect whatever territory they think they have. The territory may not even be worth protecting, but the instinct to do so is strong. You can't begin to understand office politics in these situations until you recognize that fact.

Departure of Key Figure

Let's look at each of the three catalysts of unforeseen change that we've identified. The departure of a key figure will heat up the internal politics and create a certain amount of unreasonable panic in direct proportion to two things. The first is how much and how many people owed their jobs and loyalty solely to the key figure. If many people depended on that key person for their jobs—either because they worked for him or her or because the key person could hire and fire them at will—there will be much distress when those people realize that a successor may consider bringing in his or her "own team."

The second thing about that key figure's departure opens up the question of how quickly a successor can be found. The longer the job remains open, the more likely it is that someone up the ladder will reorganize the area of power left vacant. That may have been part of the original plan, or it may have occurred to top management when the key figure left.

An organization is a dynamic entity. Even though someone previously thought vital to the organization has left, decisions must be made, business transacted, and politics continued as usual. The departure left a power vacuum, and people will automatically divide up that power even though they expect someone to be hired to fill that job. Of course, the new appointee will have to wrest the power back from the troops or else he or she won't be able to do the job. In the meantime, some of the power will go to others in the area.

The common process is for Ralph's boss (Ralph is the dear departed) to absorb the power and manage the area de facto until Ralph's successor is found. Even when Suzy Successor arrives, however, she can't get control of all the power because so much power rests on a knowledge base of the individual characteristics of the organization, which it would be impossible for her to have at this time. The knowledge base builds up over time. Furthermore, Ralph's boss can't teach Suzy about that knowledge base because he didn't know the job as well as Ralph did. Therefore, she will have to let some of the power slip through to the troops, though very temporarily.

In fact, if Ralph's superior doesn't step into the power vacuum and assume command, the troops will try to readjust the situation among themselves by dividing up the power as seems appropriate. Some of the troops will get more and some less, depending on the ability to get the job done.

A real reorganization occurs when such a long period of time has elapsed since Ralph's departure that the troops have had to informally reorganize the department, and no informal method of wrestling back control exists. This is an extreme case, but to put a manager over the department without his or her having a clear understanding of what he or she can do invites months of dislocation and generally an informal reorganization as well. This is why management may be so anxious to fill a job before the departure of a key figure. The troops also prefer that arrangement because there is no guarantee that whatever new structures management creates will be better than the old. The situation is often the reverse.

These changes have two effects on the individual. First, they create long periods of job-related anxiety, particularly as to whether the person will have a job. This refers to our initial discussion of the bottom line—hatred of job hunting. Second, the changes force each worker to defend his or her turf regardless of how much he or she wants that territory. It's almost an instinct. People who really have no interest in how the power pie was divided in their office or in their department become acutely sensitive to every nuance and change. They're afraid that those below them will try to take whatever ground they've got.

There is no evidence that the powerless are fired more often than the powerful. In fact, it's quite the opposite. The powerful people who stand out are more likely to get the ax than the faceless trolls. This is so simply because some work must get done to keep the organization alive. It's the trolls who do this work. Besides, they will not threaten the new power elite, and their jobs are not in high demand.

A Shift in the Wind
The second change agent, an organization's loss of direction, presents another set of problems that provoke panic. While the departure of a key figure is a dramatic event signaling the onset of disturbed power relationships, the loss of energy and sense of direction in an organization is more subtle and less easily placed in a time frame. For most organizations in this situation, some outside event will dramatize to everyone within what has been happening over a period of time.

A famous publisher, Ken Sharon, seemed to have a magic touch with authors. Every novel he published turned to gold. People looking at his list could see an internal consistency in the kinds of books he picked, even though the subjects ranged from the serious to the ridiculous. But everyone knew a "Ken Sharon" book when they saw one.

One day a senior editor with Sharon read in the trade press that a competitor would publish a book that the senior editor knew was the sort of thing *his* house had always done. He mentioned this, casually, to a fellow editor. From that moment on a sort of unreasoning panic set in.

A monumental importance was attached to the competitor's publishing of the novel. People in the organization felt that their role within the industry was diminished. All of a sudden they felt less competitive and unsure of what they were supposed to do. Only in retrospect could the senior editor see his observation as the triggering event. He, like others in the publishing house, felt the panic of collective recognition.

While the description of the publishing house's travail is dramatic in the retelling, we're telescoping an event into a very short time frame. In fact, it was about six months before the majority of employees had begun to feel at gut level the loss of organizational energy and to recognize their own panic.

Here again, the employee is a victim. Panic comes about not because of the individual's actions but because of organizational confusion. Nothing prepares the individual for this kind of problem. What did the secretary, assistant editor, or even senior editor have to do with Ken Sharon? Suddenly, all these people were reminded of how dependent they were on others and how little control each had over his or her individual destiny. Individual action was not enough. Working hard was not enough. Working well was not enough. Hard work did not equal success. Panic in these situations stems from that recognition.

This sort of panic occurs most often in service businesses and nonprofit organizations. These organizations tend to rely on, even attract, people who build the cult of the individual around themselves. In the case of the publishing house, the organization revolved around one person. Management is often so thin in such organizations that the person at the top really makes all the decisions, and may even produce the lion's share of the income. This makes that person indispensable. When the person goes off track, the organization feels as if things are up for grabs.

Note that this situation differs from the first situation because the key person is still in the organization. Ken Sharon may even appear productive, but the employees sense that he has slipped and that there is nothing they can do about it. If the company is publicly held, the board of directors may get into the act and attempt to pressure Ken to step aside. Alternatively, they may try to revitalize him and get him moving again.

New people are brought in from competitors and given some responsibility for reestablishing direction and raising the energy level. This produces further political dislocations because people at every rung on the organizational ladder have to assess and respond to changes in light of their own careers and power arrangements. To make matters worse, someone with whom they may have been competing in the past may now be giving them orders. Nobody is satisfied with the changes.

A director of an agency or a president of a college can cause the same panic as a drifting president of a corporation when he or she stops leading the troops and seems to be "resting." While people in these organizations might fear reorganization, they are more fearful of the lack of control that grabs them as they see the organization drifting. Since many of these people hold job security above every other work-related value, they become very anxious when that job security appears to be threatened.

Marcia, president of Good Times College, allowed her drinking problem to get out of control, and it became noticeable to those around her. At first the faculty snickered, and then individual members began to rewrite their résumés. They knew that the college as an institution was dependent on her to present the proper image. Individually they were helpless—stuck with someone who could do them more harm than good. They knew that serious financial problems would result (not to mention a drop in prestige) if she were unable to continue fund raising. This would mean a possible closing of the college or cutbacks at the very least. Cutbacks would lead to the elimination of jobs. The result was an unreasoning panic.

Change in Competitive Position
The final change agent is a massive change in competitive position. The commonest example of the political effect of a change

in competitive position is the school closings and teacher layoffs set in motion by a declining birthrate. Anyone who is able to read the population forecasts could have predicted this decline because one doesn't need to educate children who haven't been born. Still, the realization that those teaching jobs were being lost here and now, and not somewhere else, took time to sink in.

The problems of teachers who are laid off are chronicled in both the community and trade press. But there are no reports on the political atmosphere in schools where teachers are still employed. It's not just the panic of who's to be fired next but the increasingly heavy competition for both a shrinking economic and a shrinking power pie.

What happens in education is no different from what happens in business. The pattern of early departures by the best and the brightest remains consistent. The viciousness of the troops, backs to the wall and jobs on the line, is rarely matched in this situation because the bottom line is survival.

TAKEOVER

The second situation that victimizes workers is the merger or acquisition. This situation is much better known but less frequent. This is the situation that has the richest folklore and also excites the most employee fear. Think of the merger or acquisition as one country suddenly attacked by another and engaging it in a "to-the-death struggle."

During mergers or acquisitions all ordinary strategy planning goes out the window. When one company is trying to cannibalize another, all rules are suspended. No one in the victim organization has any job security. Most top management people are not honest about the risks to employees during a merger—or even just a major reorganization. During a merger, employees believe what they read in the newspaper or hear from friends about the events during other unfriendly takeovers, especially the bloodbaths and pogroms that leave many people unemployed on a moment's notice. They expect the same thing in their own organization.

Top management knows that the smartest, most productive, most ambitious employees leave first. This is especially true if they are financially strapped and can't afford even a week's unemployment. They know that a competitor will be happy to hire them. These employees may stay at least a little longer if they can financially stand the risk of sudden unemployment. Still, they realize their worth and don't see the need to suffer. They can, and will, go elsewhere.

Another category of employees will stick with the organization because they believe they're far enough removed from any real power to be immune from being fired. They usually think, foolishly, that no one would really want to fire them as long as they work hard. They are productive and don't get in anybody's way. They may think that they are not important enough to replace or incompetent enough to fire. They will be most surprised when they are let go for no particular reason. That's the thing so many people don't understand. Mergers and unfriendly takeovers are not responsive to the ordinary rules governing office politics. Those employees involved will be laid off because the new management wants it that way—that is the only explanation.

Finally, a large group of employees know that they perform only marginally. They are not sure that anyone else would pay them as much as their current employer for doing so little. They will stick to the bitter end because they have few options. These people also hate the idea of job hunting because they know they have little to offer.

Panic political situations, such as mergers, produce the most unattractive behavior in otherwise decent people. Each of the players will now find a greater percentage of time tied up with what literally amounts to playing games. The major problem is that no one individual, or even a group of individuals, can deliver. All the ordinary power relationships have been broken, and nothing inside the organization has replaced them. The real power is now outside the organization and will enter only on its own terms, when it is ready. The wait and the unknown are what really create the panic.

One outcome of this is that when someone has promised someone else support and then reneges, it has twice the repercussions it would have had during ordinary times. Failure on any individual's part is magnified by the sudden increase in the stakes. Everyone on the inside feels as though war has been declared.

While other kinds of panic situations tend to be contained within the organization, the unfriendly takeover or merger will have repercussions in the outside community. The press will report the departure of key executives with much fanfare.

A creeping paranoia infects the troops, causing a great many people to distrust people they've worked with for years. Long-time alliances are destroyed and friendships undermined. Every remark is minutely examined for implications. Productive work goes by the boards. Regardless of the midwife's skills, no new organization will be born without great pain on the part of those involved in the process. Most people know this.

As top management begins to realize how serious the threat to its power is, the individuals in the organization tend to do one of two things: Either they will fight collectively, closing ranks among themselves and putting up a united front, or they will divide and be conquered, fighting among themselves and allowing the organization to fall apart.

In the first instance, the troops will tend to fall in line behind management. Even if consensus at the middle-management level had been that top management did a poor job, if the individuals were well liked, the known will be seen as a much better bet than the unknown.

In the second instance, the troops will be completely demoralized and convinced that if they are smart, they'll leave. "Every man for himself" will prevail, and women and children will not be allowed first at anything. The leaving of the best and brightest is the exact equivalent of a run on a bank. The human working capital of the company is being withdrawn, and what is left may not be enough to sustain the organization.

Naturally, the people who are attempting to take over the organization don't want to pay dearly for something that will be in shambles by the time they can take control. They will try to control the situation either by reassuring the present employees or by moving about in secrecy. The first is a reasonable strategy; the second is ridiculous. As we've pointed out, more workers are likely to be anchored to the organization through direct discussion about the problem than can ever be prevented from leaving by hiding what's going on. If top management doesn't supply sufficient information, the troops may develop their own news sources, however much management may not wish it.

RESPONDING TO CHANGE

While all of these situations characterize the worker as victim, they don't excuse victims from fighting back for their careers and for their sanity. What this does mean is that, lacking a way to gain an advantage, they must change from offensive to defensive strategies.

The basic strategy for anyone in any of these situations is to treat the problem of job survival in the same way as one would treat one's survival if one were a spy dropped behind enemy lines. This is the first rule of survival: A spy is an information gatherer—not a soldier. If you treat all your activities as if you were a spy searching for information, you'll be better off. After all, would you put your life (career) on the line on the basis of some rumor and its implications? The internal networks heat up during panic periods, and people who ordinarily aren't much concerned about "idle gossip" get very interested. Suddenly there are many more sources of conflicting information. This means that as a spy you will have to check out each bit of information. Many an otherwise astute office politician has either overreacted or underreacted to an undigested rumor that would not even have been repeated during ordinary times.

Our research indicates that during a crisis situation the more outrageous and ridiculous the rumor, the more carefully it should be examined for a seed of truth. This is so because so many ordinary sources of information are blocked. Top management hasn't been letting much information get around, and that accounts for the shock the troops feel when a major piece of news comes through the vine. Ordinarily the rumors would have introduced the topic several times before anything definitive came through the grapevine.

Management may be using something that the troops would think outrageous to pretest a particular course of action. The top people want to know just how much opposition they can expect if they go ahead with a particular plan. All this means that the rumor that appears least valid may, in fact, be a harbinger.

A medium-sized manufacturing company was acquired by a much larger firm. The acquired firm had just purchased a very expensive computer system that was brought online just as the acquisition talks became serious. The company had a large investment in the computer and had spent months getting the system going. The eleven people who worked the system felt pretty confident that, while others might be shifted around, they'd still be there. After all, it was hardly logical to make changes in the computer operations when they were just beginning to get the bugs out of the system.

One of the eleven, Jack, heard through a friend in another company that the computer was to be sold and the department fired. Jack dismissed this as idle gossip instead of passing it along to the others in the department. His reasoning was that the company would have a hard time unloading a brand-new computer tailored to the needs of a small manufacturing firm. What he didn't know, but what several of his colleagues could have told him, was that the acquiring company had a tremendous investment in excess computer capacity. Their first act would be to get rid of the second computer. The firing of the department was a shock.

Spies listen to every bit of news, however irrelevant it may appear. So do detectives. They concentrate on complete information that needs to be sifted rather than on sitting up front. It would have been far easier on the people in the computer department had they assumed that they were expendable and likely to be treated as such.

The second rule of survival as a spy or an office politician is to keep your feelings, interests, resentments, disappointments, and strategies to yourself. Only if you are planning a corporate coup d'état do you need a large group of allies. You may not need a single ally. Your interests are easier to protect if they aren't tied up with those of others—especially when there is bound to be conflict between what's good for you individually and what's good for someone else or good for the group.

Keep in mind that when people are in a state of panic, they make very unreliable allies. You can't expect most of your fellow workers—especially those who understand what's happening— to stick to any sort of plan. This is so even if the plan is nothing more than an exchange of information. It would be foolish to develop very elaborate plans in these situations anyway because even top management can't make its plans work out most of the time.

Third, don't take any sudden action. Sudden, defensive action almost always provokes a still stronger reaction. If your boss—

pressured by those above and below him or her and feeling none too secure—takes a quick turn for the irrational worse, don't panic and respond with equal haste and illogic. Instead, try to figure out what really prompted that behavior. Your hasty response escalates the war and jeopardizes your own interests with little benefit.

Fourth, always act in your own self-interest. Being a hero or heroine and going down in flames for a principle is a mistake under ordinary circumstances. It's just plain dumb when the situation is abnormal. You're trading your job for something no one can recognize or appreciate as either ethical or sacrificial. To quit before you're sure you have another job means taking a large risk with very little potential reward. It may take you longer to get a new job than you've anticipated. Your references may be harder to get because so many people will have left the organization. It may be a problem to get any kind of severance from a company going through major upheavals. All this can leave you hanging on a limb—quite unnecessarily.

As soon as one of these situations arises, assess the risks of leaving your organization versus sticking it out as long as you can. This is never easy to do because a normally dynamic situation is made even more fluid by the heating up that occurs during crisis situations.

Your decision should be made when one of two things happens—either when you find that you are spending so much time on office politics that your productivity has dropped dangerously low or when you become so upset and nervous about what is happening that you begin to have physical symptoms, for example, breaking out in rashes or drinking and eating too much or not enough. At the appearance of any of these symptoms, bail out.

Few people realize that when you become nonproductive on a job, it's not just the danger of being fired that's acute—it's the danger of having your self-esteem decline just when you need all your reserves. If you know you're ripping off the organization or just coasting, you are giving other people nonverbal signals about this. Don't wait to be fired. If that's not a possibility, you should still leave. Either reverse the downward trend in productivity or put every spare minute into intensive job hunting. You may even have to take vacation time to job hunt. If it becomes necessary, do it. It's much better to leave an embattled organization (or any organization) on good terms than under the cloud of poor performance.

Remember that in panic situations your colleagues are going to end up in organizations all over town. They could harm your reputation when you do get a new job if they remember only your behavior when they worked with you. The word would spread more slowly if your colleagues dispersed on an attrition basis rather than in a fairly short time frame. When they're being forced out on short notice, they work harder to get new jobs, and, of course, they talk about the events that took place when they knew you.

The risks of being fired for poor performance are much higher than those of being fired for political reasons or as a result of an office bloodbath. Get out rather than get put out.

The most common outcome of panic situations is that someone at the top eventually gets enough control to reestablish some facsimile of ordinary working conditions. It can take a large organization as many as three to five years to fully restore working conditions to the precrisis situation. Turnover among employees will probably hit 50 to 75 percent before this is done. It may be as much as 90 percent. If you are facing the prospect of one of these crises, there are things you can do to make the whole process bearable until you decide whether to bail out or to ride it out.

The most important preparation you can make is to secure your internal and external information sources. This is no time to drop your membership in your trade or professional association. Not only are members of these groups sources of valuable information, but they can also provide job leads when you need them most. Who wants to wait for the right advertisement in the newspaper for a dream job? In a crisis, you need to be able to call people in dozens of organizations at a moment's notice.

Next, do your homework. Revise your résumé, update your business cards, start investigating companies at which you might like to work. At the least, being prepared to start job hunting, literally on a moment's notice, gives you a feeling that you have some control in an uncontrolled situation. Hopefully, by being ready to protect your paycheck, you'll be a more decisive person as you try to keep your job and sanity.

Be careful. Don't become a pipeline for competitors who want to know what's happening internally in your organization. You may help shape events even if you're not aware of this if you become the unofficial chronicler for your organization. People may raid the place because they believe it's so unstable. That is probably not in your best interest and certainly not in the company's best interest. Unless it's your strategy to do the organization and yourself as much damage as possible, you'll want to edit and limit the information you provide business associates.

Don't suspend your ethics, using the crisis as an excuse, even though the situation may be extraordinary. You'll feel just as guilty, and being unethical will not help the situation nor will it help you keep your job. During a panic, you're subject to more, and closer, scrutiny by those above and below you on the ladder. Someone is much more likely to detect any falling away from the company during the crisis than during ordinary times. And that is how you'll be remembered.

Limit the amount of time you spend on information gathering and rumor mongering. Despite the need for accurate information, you are being paid to work, not run Rumor Central. The higher up the ladder you are, the greater will be the temptation to concentrate on exchanging information. Stick to your job.

One of the problems people have when they're working defensively is that they rarely see opportunities for advancement that they might exploit. There are dynamic risks to be taken during crises. The problem is that if you were named acting manager or acting supervisor, that title could be removed from you as events continued to swirl in the organization. Still, the title can't be removed from your résumé, nor can the experience you've gained be taken away.

The problem of short-term jobs is really an opportunity. This will give you an excellent chance to see whether you'd like that job under more favorable circumstances. If you can cope in a crisis, you can certainly run the department under more stable conditions. If you know that there is a high probability that people will leave the jobs you'd be interested in, you may want to try politicking for one of them even in the midst of the confusion and panic. You have nothing to lose and may get from a few weeks' to a few months' excellent experience. Maybe you will luck out and keep the job when things settle down. Don't count on it. Keep in mind that another organization will value your experience, and if you must move, it should be up as well as out.

MAYBE IT'S MY BREATH

The final situation that victimizes many people is when someone or several people—perhaps even your boss—decide that they dislike you. Perhaps you know the reasons that people resent or dislike you; maybe you have no idea. You can identify personal hostility readily because you begin to feel isolated. Some of your information sources drop out. You feel that things are going on from which you're excluded.

This process of being put into isolation may be gradual, or it may occur overnight. For instance, suppose that until now you and your boss have gotten along quite well. One day the boss's boss stops by your desk and comments on what a fine job you've been doing. You are pleased and express your appreciation for the comment. Your boss observes this interchange. From that minute forward, he or she regards you with hostility and suspicion. You suspect that your boss feels threatened, but you can't see yourself discussing the situation on the basis of your horseback psychology.

Other employees in your department begin to notice your boss's abruptness and tangible hostility. Fearing for their own jobs, they shy away from being seen with anyone so obviously in trouble.

The opposite side of the coin is when you suddenly begin to resent a co-worker full time. You may have gotten along quite well with the boss until you observed the boss giving all kinds of special consideration to Sarah. Sarah is thought to be first in line for a job you thought had your name on it. You begin to loathe both your boss and Sarah, though there is no concrete reason to do so. Eventually, both the boss and Sarah will pick this up from your body language and will decide that you're a threat or simply a disgruntled employee to be isolated from the mainstream.

Resentment and hostility isolate you from co-workers whether you withdraw from them or they from you. Isolation is a crisis in office politics because it means that you have been cut off from the internal information networks. That is the ultimate victimization because it means that you will receive only the information that the organization distributes formally.

The normal response when you feel victimized is to respond, defensively. "Who needs them anyway?" It ain't so. As long as you work with that group of people, you need open communication just to do your job. It's indispensable for work satisfaction or advancement. Unless you immediately reopen the lines of communication with your boss or co-workers, or try to, you risk giving someone (your boss or his or her boss) enough ammunition to fire you.

The longer you are isolated, the more likely your performance is to suffer. The pressure is not on others to cooperate with you. They are free to choose to cooperate or not.

David had had a series of small, but irritating, exchanges with a peer. Easygoing to a fault, he found Fred's persnickety, let's-do-everything-perfectly attitude mildly irritating at first and then intolerable. He hid his hostility for a week or so and then, tension mounting, began taking shots at Fred. The boss observed the sarcasm and, not understanding the situation, jumped on David. David responded angrily while Fred looked on as innocently as possible. Result: anger, frustration, and further isolation for David.

Unless David reassesses his situation, the next blowup may be his last. Our research indicates that whether it's the boss victimizing a subordinate or one worker reacting to another, the problem is not just a "personality" problem. Both Elizabeth's boss and David are scapegoating. Whether you're the victimizer or the goat being scaped, you need to look upon personal dislikes as symptoms of job dissatisfaction. David needs to ask himself why someone else's personal style is so important that he's willing to put his job on the line to change it. In every case where we reconstructed the facts and found one person venting an unreasonable hostility on another, there was a deep-seated but repressed job dissatisfaction.

For whatever reason, Elizabeth's boss and David simply could not let their feelings about their jobs surface and deal with them. Unable to do so, both turned their focus of anger on another person and concentrated their hostility on that person. The only way the victimizer can change is to ask, "Why does X raise my hostility to such heights? What's *my* problem?" The victim needs to ask, "Is it really me? Does this person have an internal furniture problem?"

Only when you can generate answers meatier than "This person doesn't like me," will you be able to act intelligently. Very much as in a tennis match, you're going to have to break the pattern of hostile exchanges (or no exchange at all) by putting the ball back in the victimizer's court. If you're causing the problem, you have to make the first move to break out of your own rising anger.

Ask yourself "what is the single most irritating thing Fred does? Has anyone else ever done that?" This is a test of the real nature of the problem. If you've met the same problem in some other work or personal situation, you're not focused. Your problem is job-related. Knowing that, you can begin breaking out of both hostility and isolation, and can try to surface the real problems to be dealt with.

As a victim, you need to choke down your panic; act, don't react, and buy some thinking time. If you personalize your victimization (see chapter 2 on personal distancing), you'll make mistakes and cause your persecutor to escalate the torture. Divorce yourself emotionally as much as possible. Remember, it is the other person's problem. If you don't want it to become yours, you've got to put some emotional distance between his or her actions and your reactions. Otherwise, you are very likely to provoke the big blowout as you thrash around in panic.

What Elizabeth should have done was to distance herself emotionally, readjust her professional self, and begin to cultivate her boss. Had she talked to the boss several times a day, letting her know what she was doing and how, she would have had at least a fifty-fifty chance of reducing some of the hostility. But she withdrew into herself, thereby giving the boss no new information. Thus, Elizabeth helped her boss confirm her own opinions.

There will always be the rare situation in which nothing helps, just as there will always be muggings and other acts of random violence. Before you decide that you are in one of those situations, do some serious analyzing. Otherwise you risk your job and maybe your reputation and work record for very little gain. Can you afford as much pride and self-vindication as you'd like to buy? Like calories, these are totaled with complete accuracy. They may also return bearing interest. People remember the great, sacrificial suicidal leap—if only as a curiosity.

Chapter 6

Changing Jobs— *or* When Enough Is Enough

At some point in our careers, each of us reaches a point when it's no longer possible to repress the ugly thought, "I need a new job." There it is. You've said it, if only to yourself.

There may be nothing particularly wrong with your present job except that you've stopped growing. You know deep down that you're going nowhere fast. At the other extreme, you may be one step away from "dehiring," as termin. euphemistically known. You start looking around halfheartedly, asking friends if they've heard of anything. After a few weeks, you give up and—still dissatisfied—settle in again.

There is no less productive approach to job hunting or career planning. Any kind of job or career change has to begin with analysis and goal setting. What do you want to do in the long run? Why is what you're doing not likely to get you there? If you had no goals and objectives, the only logical reason to change jobs would be for more money or because your organization has eliminated your job.

If you have goals and objectives that can't be met where you are now, you need a new job. Suppose, however, that you have every reason to believe you are a rising star. You like your organization, boss, and job. One day a peer is put into the job you had earmarked for yourself. You are totally surprised. This is the third time you've been passed over despite your boss's assurances that "you're in the running." Nor is that the whole truth. The fact is that you are not promotable in your boss's eyes. Regardless of any explanations you think up or of those offered to you by your boss, other superiors, or your peers, you are not going to move ahead.

WHEN YOU'RE NOT GETTING ANYWHERE— GET OUT

The number of people tied by pride to their dead-end jobs is legion. They worry about what people will think about their leaving. These people always say, "If I leave, everybody will think it's because I wasn't promoted." But what difference does it make what people you're not going to work for any longer think? They will know why you left. It's time for you to know it, face up to it, and act upon it.

If you have a sense of failure when you realize that you're not promotable, you should also feel a sense of relief. At least you know the score. Lots of people around you don't. They feel unable to face the facts. Until you feel something besides rage and injustice at your situation, you're not in a position to change jobs or careers.

You need to feel, at gut level, that nonpromotability is purely situational. There is no person who is universally nonpromotable. A dead-end job for you might be an opportunity for someone else with a different set of values, needs, and skills. You may be floundering in a large company while you should be managing a smaller one. Look at the situation.

What are some of the reasons for nonpromotability? First, you may be at odds with the political environment as created and understood by your boss. If your performance appraisals reflect the "yes, but" evaluation, *"yes,* you do a fine job, *but* I wish you'd take charge a little bit more (or less), be more (or less) aggressive, get more (or less) involved with the troops. . ." you have a political problem. Your values are different from the boss's, and he or she does not value that difference.

Second, the people who are supervising your boss may not see you as a rising star and may prevent your boss from giving you what you want. If your boss has been told not to promote you, he or she probably will not want to tell you bluntly that that is the situation. And the chances of your boss's risking his or her own neck in order to promote you are rare.

Third, you may not have projected a leadership image—as that is defined by your boss. If you don't program your internal information network to carry tales of your successes *in the style of success as defined by your boss,* you will not be seen as promotable. According to the points we discussed in chapter 3, you have wide latitude in building an image. If you are resisting conformation to the image of success in your organization as defined and acted out by your boss, you can expect failure.

Fourth, your boss may want to keep you where you are and working hard. It might be inconvenient if you moved out of your current slot. It might make your boss nervous or threaten his or her own situation. Without you to supply ideas that your boss can claim as his or her own, the boss's job might be on the line. You may be doing too good a job. Overachievers can make life so comfortable for their bosses that they kill their own career advancement. This is especially true for many women who are executive secretaries, administrative assistants, or seconds in command.

Even if Gerry, the assistant publicity manager, asked her boss once a day to help her advance, she'd get the same answer. "I could never get along without you," her boss would say. "The department needs you." As long as Gerry buys the guilt argument that "you'd let everybody down if you left," her boss will continue to block her. The rude but very pertinent question is, Why do her boss and the department need her? Isn't the boss able to manage the department on his own? It's unlikely that such questions can be raised tactfully, but the word for Gerry should be clear: It's not in her boss's self-interest to help her advance.

Overachievers crop up everywhere. They don't just populate the ranks of executive secretaries and assistants. In every category of workers, the hardest-working, most productive people tend to get locked in. These are often the same people who don't have time for office politics. "I am too busy getting out the work to play games," they say. They aren't too busy to get deadended, however. The only way to beat this is to teach your job to a variety of potential successors, to stay plugged into the internal network, and to make your ambitions known both face to face with the boss and through the network. Most bosses care most about their own comfort and pleasure, not who ensures it. If there is somebody there able to take over and ensure that comfort and pleasure, you can be spared for advancement.

Fifth, your peers may be much more capable and better educated than yourself, and they may have better social and political skills. This is hard to evaluate objectively, but if you and they aren't pretty much alike, someone is out of step. Your peers may look better than you do. You may dress badly or inappropriately for the business you're in. Many people tend to think, especially if they don't meet the public, that dress is not important. Your most important publics are your peers and superiors. In addition to just observing the differences between you and them, go back to the temperature chart and go over the material you collected on these people. This is no time to give yourself extra credit for good behavior or a pure heart. If you're not solidly competitive, you are in trouble.

If, after evaluating yourself and your competition, you conclude that you're not going to get promoted or fulfill your goals in your organization, it's time to think about either correcting the problem or, failing that, moving on.

CHANGING YOUR IMAGE

You may decide to try to change your image. There is no question that it will be difficult to do. If your boss casts his or her opinions in cement as soon as they are conceived, you may not be able to change visibly or quickly enough to do your own career any good. Ordinarily it would be easier to move on rather than try to reorient your boss and peers. There are, however, at least two good reasons to try. One is that you may not be fully vested in your organization's profit sharing and/or retirement plan. That means that if you leave now, you can't take away any of the money the company has set aside for you. When you retire, you won't get any pension from this organization or you'll get a much smaller pension than you might have had had you stayed a year or so longer.

Let's say that in two years you'll be fully vested in the pension plan. If you leave now, the decision to do so will cost **X** dollars. You figure this, with the help of the personnel benefits planner, by subtracting the pension you'd be entitled to now from the one you'd get if you stayed two more years. Then you will have some idea of what an immediate move will cost. What is the difference if you retire at age sixty, sixty-two, sixty-five, or seventy? Do not make a decision until you see what the long-range costs will be.

The second reason to try to change your image is that you may be very happy with every aspect of your job except the fact that your career is stalled. You are happy with the company, your boss, the commuting distance, your racquetball partner, and your salary and profit sharing. It would be difficult for you to find a place in which you'd be happier overall. Change for you could be a disaster because you would be giving up a set of desirable knowns for unknowns. How much does promotion mean to you? Are you concerned about what people will think if you're not promoted, or is promotion really an important part of your agenda? Are you willing to give your present boss one more chance while you try to alter your image and change his or her opinion of your abilities? You need to think this through in writing. Sit down and write out the costs of staying where you are and then the benefits. Compare them. How much can you compromise your ambition?

You might try to change from Mr./Ms. Milquetoast to Superman/Wonder Woman in one week and end up simply jarring everybody without creating any positive attitude change. Keep in mind that people did not form a clear image of you and your abilities in one week, and they aren't going to form a new one in one week. This change process involves changing behavior over at least a six-month period. It involves a plan to do so. You do not start adjusting your outward appearance without some strategy for what you want to change.

For instance, if your boss has often remarked that you need to speak up in meetings and take a more active part, you can reasonably conclude that your new image must include being more talkative in meetings and socializing with your peers and boss more often. Look back at your performance appraisals if you have formal ones and see what developmental needs your boss identified. If you have always been told that your work is fine and that you need no improvement, you will have to change your image on the basis of the characteristics of the people who have been promoted by your boss in the past. You may need or want to get help from a psychotherapist if you have attitudes you need to change.

Certainly you can change your appearance if that's a negative point. Get one of John Molloy's* books on dressing for success and follow its advice. This is probably the easiest change you can make.

Even though you are working on your image and seem to be making headway, the greatest danger at this point is that you will keep giving your boss and the organization "just one more chance" as five or ten years go by. If you decide on the one-more-chance and image-change strategy, there are two steps you must take. First, you must set a time limit. It might be that if you aren't promoted within the next twelve months, you will find another job. Second, you must actively campaign for the promotion. Campaign means that you give as much effort as you can and that you will change your image with your boss and peers. If this is not acceptable, you must move to another job.

INTELLIGENT JOB HUNTING

If, after a few months or a year, you decide that you'll have to move on to move up, you must plan a serious, intelligent job hunt. This is no time to start reading wants ads and getting in contact with employment agencies or search firms. You may do that down the road—but as part of, or as a supplement to, an overall job-hunting campaign.

The only intelligent way to job hunt starts with thinking and planning before you do anything. Uppermost in your mind must be the realization that you were a political victim. The lesson in this is that the boss is most important in moving you—or anyone else—up. So nothing will be more important than screening and selecting a new boss who will support your ambitions.

If you go over the points of conflicts—open or hidden—you've had with your boss, you'll see areas in which your values and the boss's were in conflict. You will need to list your values and rate them from most important to you (areas where you can't or won't compromise) to least important (areas where you will

---

*John J. Molloy, *Dress for Success* (New York: David McKay Company, Inc., 1975); *The Woman's Dress for Success Book* (Chicago: Follett Publishing Company, 1977).

compromise). You'll put your five most important values on your shopping list for a new boss. If you and the new boss share those five most important values, the areas of possible conflict are much reduced. For instance, if you have certain ethical standards you can't comfortably compromise, you'll have to look for a boss who shares them. If cheating on expense accounts is taboo for you, a boss who does so won't win your empathy and respect. Be as specific as you can in identifying the values you want in a boss.

Sometimes it's easier to list the characteristics you want to avoid rather than the ones you want to find in a new boss. Either way, make sure you write them down, and make them very specific.

Depending on your level in the organization, or the level you hope to join in a new organization, you may also want to do the same thing for this boss's boss. At this point, the charts on the boss and the boss's boss, like the charts in chapter 2, may be useful in helping you discover what went wrong in your relationship with your present boss.

Many people mistake a lack of open conflict for tacit agreement. This is rarely the case. Most people don't get involved in open conflicts at work. That doesn't mean they agree.

Talk with people who know both you and your present boss and ask them to describe what they see as the problems in your relationship. This is a reality check just to make sure you're not kidding yourself. For instance, if it is the boss's stated, settled intention to promote only people who have M.B.A.s and you have consistently refused to get an M.B.A., you have finished your analysis. The only thing you need in a new boss is someone like your current boss but whose educational values are closer to yours.

Generally, people at this point say, "Going back to school is a drag—it *ought* not to matter. It's not fair to base promotion on something that trivial. I'm just as smart as the folks who've gotten M.B.A.s, and I work harder and produce more." This may be true, but it is beside the point. Your boss is never going to promote you because he or she wants people with M.B.A.s. Fairness will never enter the picture. You have two choices. You can find a new boss who doesn't think M.B.A.s are important, or you can stay in your present job without hope of a promotion.

Changing the boss's attitude in this circumstance is impossible. You could always hope for the boss to leave or be promoted and for a less rigid type to take his or her place. Still, it might be years, and you'd be waiting for something that might never happen and cannot be relied on. This would be another unknown factor.

The guiding principle in deciding whether to get out is not whether something should or should not be the case but how you can adjust your work environment to best advance your career. If you don't care, or refuse, to accept your boss's attitudes as reality, you'll have no options except to gripe about the system. This will make you monumentally unattractive to everyone around you and may eventually result in termination. It's called having a poor attitude, and it will show in everything you do.

Once you have your shopping list for a new boss, you are almost ready to begin the search. Before you hunt for a new job, you must be able to answer two questions: (1) With what kind of boss would I be most compatible? and (2) What kind of job do I want? If all you want is a promotion for doing the same thing you do now, your answer is simple. However, if in addition to changing your boss, you also want to change careers, you will need to develop a new job description.

If you need help in doing this, read *What Color Is Your Parachute?* by Richard Nelson Bolles.* It's an excellent treatment of career-planning issues. Let's assume, however, that you like the work you do and only need to change the boss and the work environment. Then you can concentrate wholly on these two factors.

The place to start looking for a new job is the trade and professional associations to which you belong. Think of them as human libraries always up to date, since people update their information at work every day. If you want to find out what kinds of bosses are out there for you to choose, this is the place to go. If you don't belong to a trade or professional association, talk to your competitors. What kinds of people manage their operations? Be discreet. You can learn to get people talking without letting them know that you're searching for a new boss. Ask for examples of management styles and values. Ask what kinds of people work for the boss. You'll think to ask whether

---

*Richard Nelson Bolles, *What Color Is Your Parachute? A Practical Manual for Job-Hunters & Career Changes*, rev. (Berkeley, Calif: Ten Speed Press, 1976).

any or all have M.B.A.s, but will you think to ask other questions about education? It may be that the boss is a high school dropout and would consider someone with a college degree too highly educated. You must ask questions that help you fine-tune your picture of your potential new boss.

If you are going to talk to search firms and employment agencies, be very specific in giving them directions in this hunt for *your* job. Don't go into all the reasons you're leaving your present job, just the ones that will help them prescreen bosses and organizations. The best way to deal with them is to tell them what you don't want. If, for instance, you don't want to commute one hour each way to work and you have no intention of moving, tell them not to call you for job interviews with companies outside your territory. It's a waste of time to talk with people for whom you would never consider working.

Expect the employment agencies to pressure you to interview even when the potential organization isn't what you want. Resist. Don't let anybody waste your time and vice versa. Your chances of getting a job through either a search firm or an employment agency are small anyway. Letting people know you're interested through your trade or professional association contacts is about twenty times more likely to produce a job and in a shorter period of time according to our research.

There are people in each organization that other members call whenever they have an opening because these key people always know who's looking and who might jump ship. Charlie will always call Jane because he knows that she keeps in touch with people and knows who is looking for what. Ask around until you find out who these people are and talk with them. Remember that trade and professional groups exist to exchange this kind of information—whatever the organization's charter might say. Job leads are an important reason for the rank and file to pay their dues.

Trade shows are another important source of leads. Imagine all the best people from a certain industry standing around all day at a trade show. They are important people. Organizations don't send dummies out to meet their prospective customers. If you were to turn up at a trade show exhibition hall during off-hours, you might be able to slip in and talk in an unhurried way with representatives of many of these companies about the kinds of things they are doing and the kinds of people with whom they work. You could tick off all the organizations you wouldn't want to work for and concentrate on meeting people from those with which you would want to interview.

Although extensive analysis looks time-consuming at first, it saves a great deal of time in the end. There is no such thing as a useful interview just for practice. You'll never sell yourself if you're not trying, and both you and the interviewer will know when it's just a game. If you are working full time and trying to interview, you need to conserve your energy for interviews that are important.

The more time you spend initially researching companies, bosses, and the political climates they create, the less time you will have to spend chasing dead ends in nonproductive interviews.

The want ads are another approach. Some people do get jobs by responding to newspaper advertisements. The lower the level of the job you seek, the more likely the ads are to be productive. That is, if you are looking for a job as a programmer, secretary, administrative assistant, and so on, want ads will produce some leads. They will, however, present problems in researching the political environment, since you'll rarely have time to make many inquiries before an interview. The better known and larger the company, the easier it is to prescreen and get information. You will always want to get some information about your prospective boss. After all, you're leaving your present job because the political climate and the boss aren't right for you. It would be time-consuming to prescreen bosses by going to work for them and quitting when things didn't work out.

The higher you are up the ladder, the more important prescreening becomes. That's because the higher you go, the more likely that your performance will be measured in terms of the judgments you make and the strategies you plan. Judgment becomes increasingly important. It will be a disaster if your boss and you evaluate each judgment and strategy according to diametrically opposed criteria.

Even though prescreening a boss on his or her values is time-consuming, it's not nearly as difficult as trying to find out who's really in charge. Let's assume that in your present situation one of the problems is that your boss is very weak. For example, Sally is a new vice-president who hasn't yet consolidated her authority. She has tried to promote you, but her nominees are often overlooked because she has political problems with her own superiors. You have looked at your temperature chart, and you now can see how limited Sally's power really is. Had you been more alert, you would have picked this up before you took the job. Sally constantly needs her boss's ratification, yet he is only a vice-president on the chart, a peer. Sally's limitation has made it impossible to get promoted without her boss's approval. Fred, Sally's boss, has no particular desire to see you rise.

Your first instinct is to generalize from this circumstance that all women bosses are powerless. This would be dangerous because although you may have worked for a woman boss once, that will tell you little about the universe of women bosses. What you might conclude, tentatively at least, is that it's terribly important to find out how much power your prospective new boss will have and be able to exercise independently before you decide to take the job. It will be too late once you're working for the new person.

Let's look at what you've learned from this experience. You now realize that when you interviewed with Sally, she seemed to be working from a script of questions with which she was uncomfortable. Someone else may have supplied the questions, probably her boss. You met with Sally only once, but twice with her boss. The boss seemed more concerned with your relationship with him than with your relationship with Sally. This may mean one of two things: Sally is not long for that job, and you may be reporting to Sally's boss or a new boss fairly soon; or Sally's boss has problems delegating work and authority. Either of these problems is fairly serious because you can't change a situation like that. It's better to avoid such problems rather than to start as a new employee in an unstable job situation.

Keep in mind that you are interviewing the people and the organization, not just being interviewed. If you want to get a feel for the political climate during an interview, you may want to ask some of the following questions.

1. *What kind of performance-appraisal system does the organization use?*

Evaluate the answer with the following idea in mind. If the organization has no performance-appraisal system, you will need to put that much more effort into screening the boss. He or she will have complete control over the way you're evaluated and won't even need to explain the criteria used in reaching a decision. If the system is very formal and all managers use it, to what degree has it been successful in identifying promotable people? You may need to put this to the interviewer as a two-part question or simply ask to see a form or have the interviewer explain the system in detail. Ask for his or her evaluation of the system. If the interviewer is scornful of the organization's system, be sure to ask why. A manager at odds with the system can cause problems for a subordinate because other managers may take the system very seriously.

If we seem to be overemphasizing performance appraisal, here's why. Any way of appraising performance has some built-in biases. What you need to find out is how well those biases reflect your strengths and ensure that they don't highlight your weaknesses. For example, if you are to be appraised under a system valuing interpersonal relations and this is not your strength, you'll get a lower rating. The fact that the system values relationships over technical skills would cause your lack of interpersonal skills to be spotlighted. Your great strength in technical areas would be relatively undervalued. You will be evaluated on your interpersonal skills even though you are being hired for your technical skills. A system that values technical skills more than interpersonal skills would highlight your strengths and mask your weaknesses.

2. *What has the turnover been in the department and job you are looking at?*

The saddest stories we ever hear are always the ones that start with "If I had known how many people had been through that job before I got there, I would never have taken it." You should have asked. If that's too assertive for you, ask personnel or check it out through your contacts. An evasive answer should be treated as a strong negative. If the interviewer becomes hostile or has defensive body language, this is even more of a negative. An organization may be riddled with management schizophrenia. For instance, it may hire one kind of employee even though it values people with very different talents. This could account for the high turnover. It's no place to be if you value your sanity.

If everything checks out politically and the organization cannibalizes only an average number of people, no one will hesitate when you ask about these points. Turnover is never an absolute measurement. If you ask, however, the interview · should be able to explain why turnover is especially high or especially low. If the explanation is sensible, fine. It's almost impossible to balance a very high turnover and a hostility on the part of the interviewer to your questions with enough positives to make taking the job a good risk.

3. *If you are looking for a promotion up front, ask how long your predecessor was in the job and where he or she has gone.*

You may also ask this question if you don't want to advance. Same information, but you evaluate it differently. If you want to move up and you find that your predecessor moved laterally rather than up the ladder, that's a negative. If you don't particularly want to advance, it's a positive or a neutral factor. Nobody can tell you what to make of the information you receive, just how to get it.

Organizations promise rapid promotions even when they know that they have a much slower than average rate of moving people up. It's foolish to take such promises seriously. You will have to evaluate the argument that the person before you didn't get promoted because he or she didn't want to move up. That might be so, but why is there an opening now? For example, your predecessor may have realized that the company kept salaries low as a result of a high turnover. They may try to hire beginners at very low salaries, knowing that as soon as those people get some experience, they'll move on to a decent job. Get examples from the interviewer of where, when, and how people have moved.

4. *Ask whether you'll have an opportunity to meet the people with whom you'll work.*

Anything less than enthusiasm for this request on the part of the interviewer is a cause for alarm. If the interviewer tells you that it's not possible or, worse, that you're the first person ever to ask, and what's wrong with you, you'd have to be aggressively masochistic to take the job. Of course, nothing may be wrong. The employees may be delighted with their jobs, well treated, and productive, but it's unlikely.

Consider the case of Len. Len applied for a job in the legal department of a major national retailer. After several interviews with the personnel department, he was introduced to the man who would be his supervisor. The interview went smoothly until Len asked if he could meet some of the other lawyers with whom he would be working. The supervisor seemed not only surprised but also upset by this request, and he turned Len down out of hand. The interview ended a few minutes later.

As Len walked out of the area, he saw Annette, a woman with whom he'd gone to law school. He asked to speak with her, and they retired to her office. She told him how terrible things were with that particular supervisor. Bitter about being passed over for promotion, the man took out his frustrations on his people. "I've only been here three months, and he's told me five times that I'm behind in my work," she said. Len spent twenty minutes with her and then left. Two days later he was offered the job. He turned it down.

Even if Len had not met his classmate, he should still have turned the job down. The supervisor's reaction was out of line. Other people must have sensed that the situation wasn't *kosher* because six months later the supervisor had *three* vacancies.

After the interview, make some notes for yourself on your impressions of the organization and its people. Keep these for use in comparing one boss to another.

It would not be possible to exaggerate the importance of research on the political climate before you take the job. As we said in chapter 1, 75 percent of the people who fail at jobs fail for political reasons. Many of those failures are preventable through research. If you go blindly into a job, you are betting at least forty hours a week of your time, fifty weeks a year, that luck will be on your side. A person who would make such a time commitment on the basis of inadequate research could not be trusted in the same town with a slot machine.

If you've left a job feetfirst—fired for political reasons—the temptation is to submerge every concern except that of getting on someone's payroll immediately. This is a mistake. You are gambling blindly that the situation you left was worse than a new situation about which you know nothing. Don't do it. It would be better to take a part-time job, to work for a temporary employment agency, to do night work at a factory, or to put in time at McDonald's than to make a second mistake. Being fired once can be explained, but explaining two or three firings will take a great deal of cleverness. You might have prevented all the the firings by prescreening.

The last thing you need to do before you decide whether or not to take a job with a particular boss is to get references on that boss. The average job hunter spends considerable time and effort trying to see that his or her references are carefully prepared and favorable. Few job hunters spend time checking on their prospective boss with similar diligence. If, once you think you're really seriously interested in a job, you begin trying to find someone who's worked recently for your prospective boss, you will have a better chance to talk to such a person than if you wait until the organization has made you an offer and demands an answer in three days.

Keep in mind that almost everybody is on his or her best behavior during interviews. This is especially true if the boss realizes that maybe he or she is a bit difficult from time to time. The theory is that there's no need to show one's warts when it's not necessary. Let the potential employee beware! No one is going to talk about his or her irrational behavior, inconsistencies, or shortcomings. This is the information you must dig out to make an intelligent decision. There are no spectacular timesavers or shortcuts.

It's not so important what these weaknesses in the boss are as long as they are not on your hot-button list. If the boss is organized to a fault but so are you, there's no problem. If, on the other hand, you are so laid back that you're practically horizontal all the time, this is going to cause friction. These small frictions poison the work environment, stunt your professional growth, and skunk your advancement opportunities.

What if, despite having done as much research as you could, having talked to people and evaluated their input and having thought through your priorities and values, you start a new job and then discover you've made a mistake? Do not panic. Self-doubt and self-recrimination won't get you a new job, and they sap your self-respect when you need it most. Get another job as quickly as you can and leave. It's that simple. Don't stick it out for a year on some harebrained theory that if you don't stay at least a year, you'll be penalized. Like other job-hunting chestnuts, it's as false as it is true. The important thing is to protect your health, your sanity, and your career.

Chapter 7

The Politics of Mentoring— *or* Searching for the Wizard of Oz

If there is one idea that has excited the upwardly mobile in the past few years, it's been the idea of a mentor. What job security was to an earlier generation, a mentor is to today's worker under thirty-five. Technically, being a mentor means teaching. In the past a mentor was a teacher who taught by example as well as in the classroom—the experience most people connect with the term *teacher*. A mentor was an exalted teacher able not only to instruct and guide the student but also to make things happen. A mentor was a combination teacher and godfather.

With the change in the late seventies from a boom economy to one that every new college graduate feared because of the perceived shortage of good jobs, greater interest in the mentor emerged. These new graduates were afraid to look for a good job, that is, one offering a good future and a good salary, for fear that one wouldn't appear. They began to focus on magic, and the search for a mentor was part of that magic.

The people getting masters' degrees in business administration talked about mentoring in their initial interviews with recruiters. As a result, the recruiters began to think that their companies would be judged on something other than opportunity, work content, and salary. Graduates have always had hidden agenda, of course, but this was a new wrinkle, and it was also quite widespread.

By 1979 even the *Harvard Business Review* had taken note of mentor mania in an article entitled "Much Ado About Mentors."* Again the emphasis in the article was on the teacher-godfather.

But none of the talk about mentors has been particularly enlightening because only one kind of mentor has been identified. The reader might conclude that either one gets a teacher-godfather or one does without to the detriment of one's career. Let's clear up that misunderstanding by looking at the five kinds of mentors available in organizations.

THE INFORMATION MENTOR

The first kind is the information mentor. This person takes a new employee and teaches him or her about the informal organization. The information mentor tells the fledgling about all the facts that all the employees know on an informal basis and that contradict the company's official handbook on personnel policies. The information mentor teaches and the fledgling learns. The information mentor may offer advice, evidence of what behaviors have worked in the past, and, most important, practical political information. This information usually ranges from when not to approach the boss (never before 10:00 A.M. on Mondays) to fairly sophisticated analyses of who relates to whom and how. An information mentor is very useful as you try to fill in the temperature chart discussed in chapter 2. The information mentor has a need to teach and the fledgling a need to learn. Because the mentor knows the survival information that a new employee needs, the information mentor gains prestige and power in the eyes of the fledgling. Information mentors frequently receive favors from their protégés as much as two or three years later in return for their earlier help.

There is not necessarily a direct relationship between the information mentor and the new employee. For instance, Al, a secretary who has been with a department of an organization for many years, might attempt to fill in his new boss, Sam. However, there are good reasons why Al might not wish to serve as Sam's mentor. Al has something at stake in his relationship with

---

*Gerard R. Roche, "Much Ado About Mentors," *Harvard Business Review* 57, no. 1 (January-February 1979): 14-16, 20, 24, 26-28.

Sam. Why should he get that very tentative and delicate relationship off on the wrong foot? Sam doesn't know Al well enough to trust him or vice versa. Al can give general or factual information, but he will probably withhold his opinions and analyses until he's more certain of the probability of success of the boss-secretary relationship.

The information mentor may be a secretary with status who acts as a mentor to keep and increase that status. It may be a worker who has no advancement aspirations and whose major contribution to the organization is the informal orientation of new employees. This person, often known as "good old Jack," doesn't work terribly hard but is moderately productive. He has been with the organization for ten or twenty years and is happy with it. He sees his work as a mentor as a positive contribution. There is a genuine altruistic spirit in many of these people, for they are helping an individual and their organization at the same time.

There are dangers with the information mentor as well as benefits. The information mentor may distort the information he or she passes along. Of course, the person who's being taught has no way of testing the reality of what is taught until he or she has been with the organization for some time. IMs tend to establish exclusive relationships with new employees one at a time. By the time the newcomer is strong enough to make his or her own decisions, he or she has probably absorbed some of the information mentor's views on the organization and the individuals within it. What makes a mentor's job such a fascinating process and what enables the information mentor to claim status as a teacher rather than as a gossip is the ability to influence and shape the newcomer. This takes place independently of the information mentor's real power in the organization. The information mentor acts out the rule that information, and the control of information, is power.

When you consider that the information mentor may work on several people simultaneously, and all of them at different levels, you can see how the information mentor influences the organization. People absorb much of the flavor of the organization through their individual contacts, not from the formal information that the organization puts out. The information mentor also benefits from the relationship even though he or she exacts a smaller price than the godfather mentor, as we shall see. The influence of the IM lies in shaping perceptions and in getting to the newcomer first, when that person's information need is greatest and his or her assumptions least formed.

Lest this sound like magic, the entire process often takes place over coffee or lunch, or across a desk in the most desultory way. The new employee sees the mentor as a fountain of very nuts-and-bolts information and will telephone or stop by to ask very basic questions. The information mentor shapes his or her responses to fit not only the needs expressed but also the ability of the person to act on, or with, the information presented. This process may go on for months or even years. The longer the information mentor has been with the organization, the more he or she has to tell. It becomes a process of providing an oral history of that particular subsection of the organization and those within it.

Recruiting an information mentor, or more than one, depends on not letting yourself get tied to any one group when you join a new organization or department. If you've been there some time and are tuned into one information network, recruiting an information mentor will mean gradually extricating yourself from this network as you try to make new internal contacts.

In addition to the stake the information mentor has in getting his or her version of events accepted as the definitive version, the IM often trades information for respect. This is likely if the person with the most information does not have much official status, for example, a secretary or an accounting clerk. If the information mentor most likely to help you is someone with low status, you are going to have to trade respect for information and to provide some ego massage as well. This is not only politically crucial, but also good human relations.

The information mentor will expect you to speak respectfully about his or her information to those in the network, no matter what you think about it. The simplest way to identify an information mentor is to see which of your peers go to whom for news or advice. In any work unit there will be someone other than the boss who provides the counterbalancing information. The boss commands, but the information mentor interprets.

Many women resent the need to connect with secretaries for information. They may feel too closely identified with the secretarial role or wish to avoid making the connection in anybody's mind. This is as useful as resenting bad weather. It's a fact of life that at this point in the managerial development of women, other women are important information connections. Without them, and excluded largely from the "old-boy" network, a woman is nowhere and thus cut off from information she needs to do her job. Women must use the natural connection with other women at every level and forgo the principle. If you're a woman, that's one principle you can't afford.

THE PEER MENTOR

The second kind of mentor in most organizations is the peer mentor. If you are a manager-come-lately and the managers around you have been in place much longer, one or more may serve as your peer mentor or peer mentors. The major difference between the IM and the peer mentor is that the peer mentor provides information and guidance as an equal. He or she sees the organization from the same perspective you do and has the same interests to protect.

The peer relationship is based on mutual interest. A peer's performance appraisal may be influenced by yours. There may be a need to get someone fully acclimated in order to shift work to him or her. There may be a genuine desire to help a new colleague. Most often, however, the peer mentor is looking for and building alliances. For example, a peer may not agree with management and may see you as a possible recruit to support his or her position. It's amazing how many people overestimate peer competition while underestimating peer cooperation. If Sam helps you now, you will owe him something down the road. In that way the peer mentor is like the godfather. His or her help has a price. On the other hand, unlike the godfather, he or she can rarely make something happen. His or her role is to inform, warn, and provide a sounding board. Peer-to-peer mentoring will end as soon as the mentor sees that the protégé is able to handle his or her job alone. The reason for this is that the mentor is not anxious to create supercompetitors, just allies.

The danger in having a peer as your mentor is that if the protégé turns out to outshine the mentor, who, after all, is also a competitor, the mentor may try to extract a higher price down the road. At the least, the mentor will be angry and bitter at having helped create someone who now surpasses him or her. In a desire to prevent this, the mentor frequently limits the help given a colleague or attempts to use information to build a friendship and hence an emotional, rather than a business, tie. Sad but true, you must be wary of receiving false information as well.

The minute the peer mentor moves from a teaching and influencing relationship to trying to build loyalty based on friendship, both relationships are in danger from the emotional tie created. Watch the emotional plays on the part of peers. You can get off track if you try to do the "right" rather than the career-protecting thing. Guilt and gratitude do not belong in the office. From a distance it's impossible to say whether it's good or bad for either of the people involved, only that a danger exists.

Recruiting a peer mentor may be less difficult than recruiting any other kind. The reason is that many companies formally organize this sort of relationship by making sure that a new manager has someone to depend on for such services as information about the company, testing of ideas, and a generous dose of company folklore. It's the organizational buddy system.

When you're very new on the job, a peer mentor can often be found by picking someone with a compatible personality and then asking that person questions. This use of questions and the seeking of advice to build a relationship works as it did with the IM. It enhances the mentor's prestige and political power because it seems that he or she must be "more equal among equals."

One corporate strategy that may kill or prevent the practice of peer mentoring is the imposition of a very competitive framework on the work environment. If each person sees himself or herself in a head-to-head competition with every other person, there will be few peer mentors. Look for another type of mentor.

THE RETIREE MENTOR

The retiree mentor is the easiest to recruit and offers you the fewest risks with the greatest and best possibility of extra benefits. The retiree mentor is often overlooked because it's assumed that upon retirement the knowledge that the retiree amassed over the years withered away. This is untrue. Cleaning out one's desk for the last time is not the same thing as cleaning out one's mind.

The retiree can offer a wealth of information on how the people in top management got there. For anyone trying to chart a career path and assess the odds of success on that path, the retiree is a guide through the maze. For instance, if you are in data processing and long to see yourself as vice-president, the formal answers that the organization gives you about your chances may differ from those the retiree gives. The retiree is a very good source of reality-testing assumptions about the organization.

The retiree provides three important kinds of information. He or she can give an oral history of the organization and the attitudes that have shaped it. The retiree can see any time bombs that may affect the future of the organization. And he or she can tell you what mistakes the people who now lead the organization made on the way up and, with twenty-twenty hindsight, how you can avoid them.

Only someone committed to an organization for a long time will want this much information. Indeed, because the retiree no longer has to worry about time, you will always get more information from him or her than you really want. However, the retiree can steer you away from unproductive relationships and areas.

Let's take the example of a woman who retired from a billion-dollar corporation, where she had been administrative assistant to the chairman of the board. She'd been with the company for thirty-five years, all her working life. A younger woman who wanted very much to rise in the company arranged a luncheon date and asked the older woman what she thought of the chances of a woman reaching the top echelon. Having no need to mouth the company line, the retiree explained that both the chairman and the president were of the "old school." Neither had much contact with the new breed of career women. Neither had working wives or daughters with careers. Both put great emphasis on entertaining graciously at home—a practical impossibility for many career women without household help. She could not see this attitude changing very much until both were retired or replaced. Both men were then in their early fifties. As long as the company was growing spectacularly and making money, there was no need to change the formula that had made the company successful. While the threat of affirmative action suits was always present, the retiree believed that the company would fight them or simply create a few tokens. Money was no object, and the best legal talent would be available.

The outlook for even a Wonder Woman was not great. This ran counter to every bit of information the company had distributed. No prudent manager currently employed by the company would have told a woman employee at any level what the retiree said. Yet when the younger woman looked at the kinds of jobs women held in the company, the retiree's analysis had the ring of truth. They were employed either in staff positions or as technical specialists—not a place from which top management has been plucked in most organizations. There was one woman in sales—the site of top management training. She was reputed to be doing adequately but not playing a starring role. She was also said to be dissatisfied with her exclusion from the "old-boy" camaraderie that is so important in sales.

The younger woman gave all this information a great deal of thought. What struck her was the difference between how the company looked in the historical perspective supplied by her retiree mentor and how it looked in the official and formalized folklore of how people moved up. She did not leave the company, but she began working on moving into sales. She began to question the kinds of opportunities available to women. She might have gotten into top management except that, as she was in the process of changing the company, another corporation spotted her through a recruiter and made her an offer she couldn't refuse. Without the mentor, the level of risk this employee might have taken would probably have been lower. Once she got a feel for the company's real beliefs, she decided that, since she would have to move on anyway, there was no risk in a little judicious agitation, if only to make things better for the women who would follow her.

Of course, the retiree was the sort of person any new employee would appreciate. Unfortunately, everybody who retires from an organization won't bring this woman's unique experience and perspective to the task. Some will have been in dead-end jobs with no chance of an overview. A major danger is that the retiree will not have seen the broad outlines but only one particular point of view. You won't get an overview; instead, you will learn how the retiree thought the company should have been run or his or her favorite version of what might have been.

The nice thing about retiree mentors is that the larger the organization, the more of them there are from whom to choose. The motives of the retiree are not complex. The ones who have an ax to grind will talk in the hopes of converting you and hence influencing the organization indirectly. Many will talk because someone will listen. It gives them a sense of their own importance. They like being appreciated for what they know and have done—as who does not?

Recruiting a retiree mentor means tracking down the people who've retired from your working group. The information mentor should be able to give you the names of some people still in the area. Failing that, ask personnel. They will know who has retired recently and may even give you these people's names and telephone numbers. Wanting to meet retirees is often seen as an act of altruism. If the personnel office gets huffy, contact the local branch of the Gray Panthers or the American Association of Retired Persons and see if such organizations can be more helpful.

Some of your fellow employees who are older—say, over fifty-five—should be able to give you names. Assume that if you tap into the network of retired people at any point, you'll be able to use it to find someone from your immediate area or a similar area.

Expect to spend some time with the person you recruit and to be honest with him or her as to what you want and why. Not everyone retires voluntarily from an organization, and you may have found someone with an ax to grind. If that's the case, don't be distressed. Hear the retiree out—you may learn what to watch for in the future. Younger workers often have a difficult time listening to a seventy-year-old with unlimited time to tell every detail. It would be a mistake to rush the person. Only with every nuance and detail can you hope to form an intelligent plan or judgment.

Expect that it may take several months of effort to locate the right person and get that person talking. Remember also that it's important for you to encourage the person to talk at length rather than just fire questions at him or her. You'll be greatly rewarded not only by the information but also by a savvy you might not have expected. People don't age in their heads—just in their bodies.

THE COMPETITIVE MENTOR

The fourth kind of mentor is the competitive mentor—someone who works in your job, or in a similar job for another organization like yours. This is a mentor you can meet at trade and professional organizations and who will provide unique, valuable insights into your own organization.

First, let's be clear that you and a competitive mentor will never be exchanging trade secrets. That's illegal, unethical, and, from a career-planning standpoint, suicidal. Instead, the competitive mentor adds another dimension to the picture you're trying to complete of your organization and the people within it.

It's a mistake to assume that IBM salespeople and Xerox salespeople never cross-pollinate. First, who could possibly be more interested in IBM than people who work for a company in direct competition? Second, no one else could possibly be as sympathetic and insightful into the problems you face and the kinds of political situations you meet than people who do exactly what you do for a competitor. They have many of the same problems and frustrations.

The competitive mentor can swap rumors with you about your own organization that you'll never hear internally. For instance, if your boss, the sales manager, has been playing footsie with another company and seems likely to leave and become its vice-president of sales, he or she may have covered all of the networks internally so that no one has even an inkling. Still, even if he is extremely street smart, he or she may not have thought about the competitors. A person you know as a competitor may mention hearing that your boss has been talking with XYZ. That bit of information can be invaluable if you decide to run for your boss's job. You can begin early before potential internal competitors know there's a contest. As said in chapter 2, advance information buys time for planning.

The competitive mentor can even tell you how something is done or organized at his or her company. He or she can help you see a different perspective. In political wars, when your job is shaky, the relationship you've built up can even help you get an interview or a job at his or her company.

The nice thing about competitive mentors is that this is a more equal relationship. You don't owe anything down the road because you are paying as you go with information in kind.

Nonprofit organizations as well as profit-making ones have competitors. If there are two adoption agencies in town, regardless of the constituency each sees itself serving, there are enough similarities for you to find a competitive mentor. The same is true of government agencies. As long as there are two of anything, there is a competitive situation even if all the employees deny this.

THE GODFATHER MENTOR

The final kind of mentor is the godfather mentor. This kind of mentor receives the most publicity, excites the most envy, and is most desired by new workers.

The godfather mentor is someone who not only can teach, inspire, and orient but also can make things happen for his or her protégé. In no other relationship with a mentor is there such a close intertwining of business and emotional needs and payoffs. If you looked at this relationship under a microscope, you would immediately see that it's a symbiotic relationship, not an altruistic one as are the other relationships between mentors and protégés. The godfather needs the protégé almost as much as he or she is needed by the protégé; this is definitely a two-way relationship.

The motives of the godfather are uppermost in creating the relationship. He has something he wants passed on in the organization. No understanding of the godfather mentor is possible without that keystone. The godfather is looking for a perpetuation of his ideas in a kind of corporate immortality. The idea is that if he helps shape and boost a real comet within the organization, there will be a payoff in seeing his ideas influence the organization.

The godfather and protégé discover each other in one of two ways. Either there is almost instant recognition of a chemistry between them or, as soon as they work together, they recognize that they are kindred souls. This chemistry is true of man-to-man, man-to-woman, and woman-to-woman relationships. The protégé may have either complementary or very similar skills. We have researched relationships with both. One similarity we found in all of the relationships was a shared sense of humor. This kind of close working relationship demands people skills of a high order, particularly a negotiating ability, assertiveness, and intellectual and emotional honesty.

The protégé was almost always brighter than his or her peers and was generally thought to be brighter. A true godfather does not attempt to protect a marginal performer. He is far more likely to pluck off the one sure success in a group and train that person. In cases of women whose mentors were men, the women were very ambitious and were thought to be equally as bright as, or perhaps brighter than, their male competitors. They performed extremely well in areas that both the organization and the godfather rated as hard work. If the women had personal lives, they subordinated them to their work.

There was no blood relationship between the godfather and the protégé. Most surprising, in the case of male godfathers and female protégées, while there was often deep affection and respect, only in one out of twenty cases was there a love affair. If anything, a love affair seemed to hurt the working relationship rather than enhance it. While the idea of a woman sleeping her way to the top has wide acceptance in some business circles, it is a liability in the relationship between mentor and protégée. It diminishes the woman's ability and bases her success on her physical rather than on her business prowess. It also diminishes the godfather, as his protégée's success is compromised and his taste questioned. The women who were protégées were most anxious to protect themselves and their mentors from even the suggestion of a physical affair and seemed anxious to be involved with the godfather's family as a family.

One tip-off that the relationship was business and nothing else was the frequency with which the wives of the godfathers spoke well of the protégées. There was no hint of insecurity, jealousy, or envy. Even in the case of godfathers who divorced their wives or were divorced by them during the period of their relationship with a protégée, the protégée's role was never seen as a factor—even by a wife bitter over another woman! The protégée was rarely the culprit.

In the few cases in which women were having affairs with their godfathers, the attraction was almost always a result of the commonality of interests, shared ambitions, and personality compatibility that had been the basis for their relationship at the start. She was not "using" him or trading sex for advancement. The relationships in which a woman saw herself as using him or trading sex for advancement were not really relationships between mentor and protégée. He might be seeing that she earned more money or got a bigger title or more responsibility, but the relationship lacked the essence of that of a mentor to a protégée because he was not teaching her and helping her improve her business skills.

The woman was also rarely identified as the best and the brightest. Women so identified felt no need for a "user" relationship. The relationship had the same pluses and minuses as any love affair. There was no evidence that the relationship between mentor and protégée was greatly affected by the end of the physical affair. Both parties continued to work together. What would end the relationship was the marriage of the godfather to the protégée. One or the other, but usually the protégée, would then leave the organization for a job elsewhere.

In all relationships of a male mentor and a male protégé, the younger man tended to be ten to twenty years younger. Both shared the same life-style and educational background. Sometimes the protégé seemed almost a clone. All such relationships were so close to the norm and so expected that there was almost a routine quality to them. The protégé was not always the very brightest newcomer. Sometimes he was the most likable or the most eager to learn. Regardless of these factors, the mentor would always describe his protégé as the "most" of something. There was none of the risk in the all-male relationship that characterized a male-female relationship. As a result, the men rarely gave the same intensity to the relationship.

The godfather relationship tended to continue over extended time periods, whether it was man-to-woman, woman-to-woman, or man-to-man. We found few woman-to-man relationships, though it can be expected that, as more women move up the corporate structure, these possibilities will increase. The average length of time of these relationships was from five to ten years, and many lasted as long as fifteen to twenty years. No other relationship between mentor and protégé was so long-lived with the same degree of involvement. The other relationships started up, peaked, and returned to a very low maintenance level. They might have had periods of high activity, but these were always intermittent.

Having a godfather mentor presents the most dangers to both the godfather and the protégé. If the godfather should suffer a sudden political reverse, the protégé will suffer as well. Because the two have formed a close bond, it will be difficult for anyone else in the company to see them as unconnected. The result puts the career of the protégé in the hands of the godfather even in situations in which the protégé is not directly involved.

A second danger—particularly, but not exclusively, in the case of the male mentor-female protégée relationship—is that the protégée may become both so dependent on and so attached to the godfather that she will be reluctant to end the relationship, even though she sees clearly that it's time to move on. Remember that these relationships often start as—or may turn into—personal as well as professional relationships. Despite the wish to be cold-blooded, practical, and professional, turning one's back on the person who has helped you is very difficult. It's a wrenching experience and one that most protégées put off as long as they possibly can.

The godfather may change and go off in a direction that the protégé does not want to follow. The protégé, for his or her own career advancement, may need to end the relationship at this time. This will be twice as painful as the situation in which the relationship is ended because of the need simply to move on. If the relationship ends over a values or goals conflict, it will be much more painful than if the protégé simply needs to "leave the nest." The values conflict implies a rejection of what the mentor represents, which is a more painful situation for both parties.

You are correct if you think that this relationship seems to have overtones of parent-child relationships. In fact, the godfather is almost always a father figure to the man or woman he helps. The "godmother" will be more of a role model and political mentor than a mother. This is true probably because there are at present so few women at the level necessary to become godmothers; in addition, few of these women are biological mothers.

The more confident the protégé becomes in his or her judgment, and the less dependent on the godfather for help and information, the more he or she will want to divorce himself or herself from psychological dependency on the godfather. As the protégé strikes out independently, he or she will need the godfather less. The godfather will experience a sense of loss as his role diminishes.

Frequently, the protégé ends up giving in to the godfather and doing things the godfather's way. If the protégé gives in too often because it appears the political or expedient thing to do rather than because he or she was logically convinced, the relationship eventually falls apart with pain and bitterness on both sides.

The godfather might pick a protégé who did not want his help. It is also possible for a protégé to seek help from a godfather who doesn't want to work with the protégé. Both circumstances occurred fairly often in our studies because of the dynamic nature of the organizations.

Even though the godfather-protégé relationship is not free of dangers and problems, most people who've played either or both roles think that it has been the greatest competitive boost to their careers. The godfathers themselves talk in terms of enhanced prestige at having discovered the organization's savior. They feel that they've developed someone who has helped the company in one particular area or they feel that they have developed someone who added to the organization's talent bank. Protégés listed an improvement in the quality of their work life, a belief that someone was guiding their efforts, and enhanced prestige as a result of being known as someone's protégé. In the end, most of them saw the relationship as well worth its dangers.

Recruiting a godfather is not as difficult as you might think because of the mutual needs we discussed. The first thing you must do is survey who in your organization might make a suitable godfather. This person will be at least two and possibly three levels above you. If not, the mentor will not be able to push your career or intervene on your behalf. Certainly a mentor only one level above will not be able to protect you.

The people you identify as potential mentors must be scrutinized for three qualities: (1) They must have the ability to teach as well as the patience and desire to do so; (2) they must be secure as individuals—an insecure mentor who plays with and feeds from your ego is too horrible to contemplate; and (3) you must genuinely like that person and admire what he or she has done. Don't try to fake this. The godfather-protégé relationship is a most personal as well as professional one; it's impossible to fake it over the long term. Do not even try to establish a relationship with someone you do not like.

Once you have picked several likely targets, it's time to use your information network to see if any of these people have already established a relationship as mentor with someone else. In the end, you'll probably find one or, at most, two possibilities. Building a relationship of protégé to mentor with either one will depend on your ability to build any kind of a relationship to start with. You can work on only one person at a time. You will need to make this person aware that you exist, and that you and he or she share some of the same values. There are a number of ways to do this, but two are normally very successful.

As a matter of course, you will have gathered as much information on your target as you can, both on his or her professional as well as private life. One of the tactics that has worked for many people is to cut out a clipping that either strongly supports or strongly disagrees with the views of your target and give it to your target. Naturally, you will take this clipping from a publication that the target does not read regularly. That precludes the *Wall Street Journal, Forbes, Fortune,* and other common business magazines. It might include the *Manchester Guardian,* regional publications, or trade publications other than those from his or her own groups. An English business magazine is great and can usually be counted on to say something outrageous.

A second way is to find an opening that enables you to ask for career advice from your target. This cannot be trumped up. You must be sincere in wanting the target's advice and be prepared to act in some way on it. You cannot seem to be going above the head of your boss to this person, or you will be in trouble with your boss long before you've secured a mentor. It's obvious that if you try to do this on company time and in the office, you are going to have a problem. Therefore, it's most important that your research should have turned up some information on the kinds of meetings the target regularly attends that are business related. Women especially must confine their casual encounters with the target to business occasions. Otherwise the relationship may not develop along business lines—or be perceived as a business matter by others.

It may take you from six to twenty-four months to really connect with your target and establish a godfather-protégé relationship. It may be a bust, in which case you'll work on another connection. This sort of relationship develops over time and really can't be forced or rushed. If the chemistry isn't right, it will never fulfill your expectations.

Given the difficulty of establishing a relationship with a godfather mentor and the relative ease of establishing other kinds of relationships with a mentor, it's important to recruit other mentors while you're working on a godfather. In any case, your career won't be built entirely on a relationship with a mentor. You need to work all sides of the street as much as possible. Keep in mind that no one kind of mentor is the answer to all problems at all times or even at one time.

The risks of developing any kind of relationship with a mentor include the emotional ties that you may establish as well as the problem of extricating yourself after the relationship has run its course. All withdrawals and divorces are painful. You should expect that if you've received this kind of assistance early in your career, you'll need to return it down the road by becoming a mentor for others.

Chapter 8

Extraordinary Politics— *or* Out of Sorts in the Office

Sex in the office is one of the questions most often confronted by career counselors—about one out of every five or six questions asked. It's certainly one of the juicier aspects of office politics, but it's still a political rather than an interpersonal issue. At least it's political when the dramas are played out in full view of people in the office.

There are other special political situations that are not often seen as political issues. In this chapter we'll examine five of them: sex in the office, women and minorities, small organizations, very young workers, and workers over forty years of age. We want to deal with each group as an extraordinary political phenomenon and look at both problems and solutions of each situation. We've grouped them because all of them share one characteristic. Persons in each of these situations confront office politics at a competitive disadvantage because they are working under a set of assumptions that are not shared by those around them.

SEX IN THE OFFICE

Sexual politics is not sexual harassment. Sexual harassment is a legal as well as a political problem, and it should be handled with the aid of a good lawyer. It occurs when either a man or woman tries to secure sexual favors from someone (possibly a subordinate) in exchange for career advancement (or nothing at all) and refuses to take no for an answer. Clearly, there's no harassment in one hint or one offer. The harassment arises as a result of insistent repetition. If that's your problem, consult a lawyer without delay.

Sex in the office becomes a political issue when two people, regardless of their marital status, have an affair. It will almost always affect their careers, despite their persistent efforts to maintain discretion and secrecy.

Let us suppose that Doug and Julie are auditors for a large accounting firm. They are sent to East Cupcake, Iowa, to audit a corn producer—a job that will require their presence in East Cupcake for about six weeks except for trips home over weekends. Occasionally the partner in charge of the engagement, as jobs in accounting firms are known, calls on the telephone or comes out for a day. Otherwise they are on their own.

Doug and Julie are about the same age, single, and dedicated to rising in the firm. After a few days of working all day, returning to the motel for dinner, and then each going off to his or her own room to watch cable television, they decide to go to a movie. After a few evenings at the movies, they exhaust the local supply. They now spend some evenings playing backgammon or gin rummy. They talk. Eventually, they may decide that they like each other. They have an affair. They may even decide to get married.

At the point that they decide to date—much less to have an affair—they are going to run afoul of office politics. They are involved in what Margaret Mead called corporate incest. As we said before, any such relationship is an exclusive and excluding relationship. Doug and Julie are acting out exactly what people want to believe happens between men and women on the road. The fact that they are both single is immaterial. The facts are not nearly as important as what members of the upper echelon in the firm think.

According to our research, the upper echelon will think that Julie should have said no. She, not Doug, will bear the brunt of the firm's displeasure. In other words, the double standard is alive and well in business. The choice for Julie tends to be fairly stark. How much is Doug worth to her? Is he worth a partnership in the firm? Indeed, that may be the price. Not that the managing partner will ever call her in and say that he really feels that nice girls don't or shouldn't. That would be both blatant and illegal.

Affirmative action has not changed the double standard; it has simply made it more difficult to talk about. Remember that if a firm wants to deny anything to anybody, it will find a way. A firm can be as arbitrary, unfair, and irrational as the people within it with the power to enforce their decisions. Men sometimes have problems in organizations where affairs are thought to be catching or where the undercurrent is very puritanical. In most cases, however, it's Hester who wears the scarlet *A,* not Dimmesdale.

In sexual politics women usually lose, but the risks and the price are quite high overall. Corporate incest creates problems for the participants and focuses attention on the wrong issues. It does this in the same way that "As the World Turns" focuses on sexual interaction to the exclusion of work or intellect. It's human nature. Why does Rosemary Rogers sell books? In theory, any worker's private life should be private. In fact, it rarely is.

In the corporations we surveyed, no management took a truly laissez-faire attitude toward corporate incest despite some talk about defending privacy. They said one thing and did another. Women were more likely to bear the brunt of organizational disapproval because the people who punished or withheld benefits tended to be men. But women in top management were no less disapproving of other women involved with co-workers.

Married people having affairs with single or married people in the office excited greater disapproval but less action. As one top corporate official said, "Well, it goes on sometimes, but it's not a big deal." Apparently such behavior is thought to carry the seeds of its own punishment.

One thing all the managers we surveyed agreed on was that there was no way that any two people working together could have a close relationship—even purely platonic—without other people knowing about it. The internal network works efficiently!

Most people, at whatever level, expressed nothing but contempt for the secretary who sleeps with her boss or the young male worker who sleeps with his female boss in the hope that this will speed her or his advancement. Interestingly enough, people felt that co-workers would "take care" of these people. Perhaps these people meant isolating the offenders. We didn't get a definition—just the statement that they would be taken care of.

It would take a psychiatrist to explain the continuing attitude of management toward the double standard and why people with no stake in the outcome have such extreme reactions to other people's semiprivate lives. The point for the politically astute is to recognize the risks. Personal distancing, which we discussed in chapter 2, includes corporate incest among the political taboos. Of course, not getting to the incest stage means not getting involved at an emotional level at all.

However, since this philosophy usually provokes howls of rage both from those currently involved and those wanting to be, keep in mind that the risk is measurable. It's a matter of how much risk and the costs of levels of risk. It's not difficult to measure top management's attitude toward this sort of thing. If your company is extremely reluctant to have just one man and one woman travel together on business versus four or five people together at a trade show, you can pick up this attitude. If your immediate supervisor or boss's boss is concerned about the corporate image or about setting an example for the troops, you can expect him or her to take close relationships between employees seriously. Since no one will talk openly about attitudes toward these relationships, you'll have to infer how high the risk of such behavior can be. Don't plan to discuss this openly with your boss—however close the working relationship may be otherwise—because you'll be trying to talk rationally about someone else's gut responses. The power is on the side of management; the choice is on the side of the participants.

In the old days—say, five or ten years ago—office affairs tended to be between male superiors and their female underlings. In most organizations, that has changed so that an occasional female superior may take a "biblical" interest in a male underling. Even in these cases, the woman will have more problems with her peers and superiors than the man. People in the office may even think he's being victimized. (That may be!)

Nobody can tell anybody with whom to fall in love, but anybody contemplating such a maneuver should think about the consequences before he or she gets involved. There is no politics-free working environment, and judging from our research, there are no politics-free love affairs either.

WOMEN AND MINORITIES

At the same time as we researched sexual politics, we also tried to investigate the special problems of women and minorities in organizations. Minorities have an involuntary problem, inherent in the very essence of their being. But their political problems stem from two roots. First, they tend to have very inadequate experience in teamwork. Second, they tend not to believe in the cooperation to which most organizations pay both lip service and real allegiance. Some organizations truly value and practice teamwork, while others just talk about it.

Women have been, until very recently, excluded as children from most team sports. The result has been an inadequate understanding of the need to be team players. This has been well documented by a number of writers, notably Hennig and Jardim in *The Managerial Woman* (New York: Anchor Press, 1977). Minority men have had little reason to think, even if they've had a gread deal of experience in team play, that the majority white society is going to allow them—much less encourage them—to join the organizational team.

Although they arrive at the conclusion from different bases, women and minority men agree that anything they get will be something they get for themselves. They don't expect cooperation or support from peers and superiors to the same degree that white males do. They are Calvinists—rugged individualists who have seen nothing in the past to suggest that white males were anxious to cooperate with them. They knew themselves to be absolutely excluded from the power centers in organizations and saw themselves as individuals knocking on an unopened and unopening door.

As a result, these groups tended to develop support outside the organizations from other organizational loners. They did not seek team membership within the organization, for they saw no evidence that they would ever receive it. Naturally, when now accused of not being team players, these people are both surprised and outraged. As one woman said, "I'm still not included in lunch with the boys, even though they invariably talk business. If I insist on joining them, I'm pushy. If I don't insist, it's because I'm not a team player." Blacks and Latinos report the same mixed reaction. "Why doesn't Harvey join us for lunch? Why should he need to be asked?" the boss will say. Well, that black man is just preventing rejection.

Teamwork is a technique that, like personal distancing, is supposed to make the competition less individually competitive and therefore less painful. In the end, most important decisions are made by one person and ratified by a team—not made altogether in concert.

Still, if a boss, your boss, for instance, is wedded to the teamwork theory, he or she is not likely to be divorced from it by your pointing out the problems involved. In fact, to attack teamwork as a hypocrisy is to invite a spirited defense. What can the boss say?

If you are in an organization that puts great store on teamwork, you'll really have to come to grips, at the very least, with developing the team player facade. Start by banishing the word *I* from your vocabulary except in instances when *we* would be wildly inappropriate. For instance, "We are going to the men's room now" is wildly inappropriate—but short of that, use *we,* especially when referring to projects you've worked on.

Give up the idea that talking over ideas with others, even though you've already decided on a course of action, is a waste of time. It isn't. It casts you as a team player concerned about involving others. It also sells each of the people you talk with a piece of the risk of implementing an idea. This doesn't mean that if someone doesn't agree with you, you don't do it. It simply says to your co-workers that you value what others think. Even though people see through what you're doing, they will value being asked. It is a high form of flattery.

Keep the individualism to a minimum when it doesn't count anyway. If you're to infiltrate the old boys' network, you're going to have to work at it in some way every day. You don't have to make it a full-time career. If you have coffee with the old boys, you can skip lunch that day. But every day you've got to reeducate them to see you as part of the group. Remember that, in the final analysis, they can't withhold membership. The organization confers membership by the mere act of hiring you.

These people can't run a For Members Only group on company time and at company expense. If that's too gutsy a rationale, you may want to tell yourself that your career and advancement depend on helping the old boys break their old, destructive habits. Besides, you have something to offer. Management and upward mobility are not gifts—they are taken in competition from others who want the same things. If you're timid, you'd best look for some kind of work that rewards timidity. (This will be difficult to find.)

Don't try to change attitudes; change behaviors. It's unlikely that in our lifetimes we'll see full acceptance and respect for women and minority managers. The people with the power to confer that respect and acceptance are still holding on to their old power and prerogatives tenaciously. By giving in to groups that serve as challenges to the established power structures, old-timers may feel they are letting the company down. If you try to change the way these people *feel* about you personally or about your group as a whole, you'll frustrate yourself and everybody else. Instead, change behaviors and let the attitudes take their time in changing.

Paul Dickson, writing in *MBA* magazine, says that one of the rules of the game is "Never Try to Teach a Pig to Sing; It Wastes Your Time and Annoys the Pig."* When you try to change attitudes, you are trying to teach the pig to sing and the pig will get very annoyed.

From a political point of view, it's much better to make it uncomfortable for people to express their prejudices orally than to try to change opinions through logical argument. If you try, you're trying to argue rationally with someone's irrational, deep-seated feelings—ones he or she may not even be fully aware of. It can rarely be done. It's less difficult, however, to make people who call women "gals" or "girls" or black men "boys" feel very uncomfortable.

Many white people have a gut reaction against having black people live in their neighborhoods. The difference between now and ten years ago is that today they'd hesitate to voice that prejudice in the company of people (black or white) whose respect they need or want. It's just not socially acceptable. Changing people's behavior takes time, but it can be done without alienating your boss or other power sources. It requires the abil-

---

*Paul Dickson, "Never Try to Teach a Pig to Sing; It Wastes Your Time and Annoys the Pig," *MBA*, December 1978-January 1979, p. 38.

ity to control your own expressions and body language to the extent that when someone makes an unacceptable remark, you don't overreact. For instance, a woman who doesn't want her boss to call her his "gal" should tell him at once. "I'd prefer if you'd refer to me as your assistant rather than just as a gal. All the *women* in the office think it just sounds more professional." To overreact is to call attention to the faux pas and to escalate the risks. Underreaction is much more effective and has less risk. Most people who overreact try to get some apology or concession from the other person. This tends to escalate the war. It is rarely effective.

Don't expect to like the team concept at first. As with any new behavior, it's going to take some time for you to join the team. Just as you're working on other people's attitudes by changing their behaviors, work on your own. If you've always depended on yourself to look after your own interests, you'll have as much trouble adjusting to teamwork as if you were joining a labor union. Expect this and treat it as a temporary condition. If the organization you're with is too far into groupiness, change organizations. You'll never find an organization that is totally opposed to teamwork, but there are degrees in between the extremes. How much committee work and group thinking can you stand? Analyze this and your decision will be simple.

Remember that the more you differ from the norm, for example, if you're a black male in a predominantly white male group, the more you'll have to show that you accept the group values. It's not just winning acceptance that's important but also showing that you're not opposed to group values—that you can live with the things the group believes. If you can't, you leave. This acceptance can be passive—no one expects wholehearted endorsement. After all, you are different. Your background, if not your education and class, are different. You can make a contribution that's important by helping to build a bridge between your values and theirs. Without the bridge you're a misfit. Remember that organizational life is built along military lines. Military institutions demand acceptance of group norms even if it's a surface acceptance.

Your gut response will probably be to do things yourself or to decide alone what to do. It must be your considered response that you can change.

SMALL ORGANIZATIONS

In small businesses (those with fewer than fifty employees), the politics is both more potent and more volatile than in larger ones. It's so much easier to know almost everything that goes on and to react to and hear reactions about each isolated incident. A magnification occurs. Every time a small event occurs—one that in a big organization would pass without much notice—a small organization experiences a collective shudder. Everything seems bigger because the survival of the whole depends on the efforts of fewer people and on still fewer key people.

Since small businesses are frequently owned by the founder or the relatives of the founder, people who work for them live with a gnawing insecurity. The XYZ Tool and Glue Works could fail if the owner died, whereas many people could die at General Motors before the ordinary worker felt the effect.

The founder-owner of a small business tends to keep much more of the power to himself or herself. There is rarely a shared management concept. If he or she collects the voices from middle management, there is still a felt need to "go along with the boss." The creative, entrepreneurial drive that helped the founder get the business started was partly an unshakable belief in his or her own judgment. As a manager, rather than founder, it makes him or her rigid. Even when the lieutenants see the owner making bad judgments and the business failing, they rarely feel able to offer advice or to interfere. It's often the cult of the individual. A business managed as someone's special toy is not going to inspire faith in the security-minded. It tends to appear that decisions are arbitrary and can't be appealed.

Employees not related to the owner find nepotism hard to handle. They watch what they say among themselves, and usually the organization divides into two networks: the family network and the nonfamily network. The family members are never trusted by the outsiders because each one may be a direct pipeline to the owner.

Employees in small businesses are treated more paternally than in larger ones. There is a warmer atmosphere and frequently a sharing of family stories, attendance at weddings and funerals, and a certain "family" spirit. This creates a much more personal work environment, which may counter the insecurity people feel about the longevity of the business. It also breeds a certain conformity, since there's no anonymity. It's harder to lose oneself in the crowd or cover up any problems.

Small companies tend to give bonuses in very good times and to expect employees to take cuts and stick it out in bad times. Loyalty to the owner is expected. Indifference, which can be masked in larger organizations (along with a lot of other things), can't be tolerated in a small business. It's an emotional threat to the owner. He or she gets much ego satisfaction out of his or her role as owner, provider, father or mother figure for the employees. Without the ego balm provided by loyal employees, some of the zest of power is gone. It's unlikely that the merely competent but emotionally uncommitted employee will last. This makes the selection process of new employees self-selection. Either you like, trust, and admire the owner and want to work personally for him or her, or you don't. It would be very poor career planning to go to work for a small organization if you did not have those feelings for the owner or to stay on after those feelings had departed. It would be impossible to hide your real feelings, and they would be a continued affront to the owner.

While there is an expected emotional conformity, there is little conformity in other areas. The employees may differ in their individual preferences, tastes, and life-styles along a much wider continuum than a larger organization would tolerate. Alcoholism, misanthropy, sexual preferences such as homosexuality, and older, even less productive employees—all will be tolerated in ways that big organizations would find unnecessary. Since the emphasis is on a kind of personal loyalty and commitment, once past that emotional barrier, practically anything else is OK. This fits in with the family concept. As long as you produce what you are supposed to produce, and a bit more, you can deviate from the norm at will. This is the chief attraction of small businesses for people who don't want to fit into the larger company life-style. The chief disadvantage, in most people's view, is that most decisions are arbitrary, often unreasonable, even whimsical. It's useless to argue the legal niceties of discrimination with small business owners. They aren't concerned because they feel sure the government prefers whales to trout. "Eagles don't hunt flies," they say, and do whatever they please.

Small businesses, unless they get rid of the founder or get some managerial rather than entrepreneurial expertise, tend to go up like rockets and then stagnate. They can be great places for the young to learn about a particular activity or business but tense places for older people who worry about security.

VERY YOUNG WORKERS

The worker between eighteen and twenty-four has special problems, too, though these problems are more a function of age and inexperience than of cultural background. Many times the beginner has a much romanticized notion of how quickly things move in an organization. Reformist zeal has not died in the young—it's simply gone underground. The legacy of the sixties has moved into organizations, but it's guerrilla warfare, not open rebellion.

All of our research indicates, as we said in chapter 1, that the postwar generation has no institutional loyalty. Without analyzing this deeply, it's easy to see the impact of this on organizational politics. The young worker doesn't take the same pride in the organization as an entity that the older worker did in the past. As one young man said, "Who cares what name is on the check as long as the bank will cash it?" He puts the case in the extreme. Most workers aren't that indifferent. It's just that they have little tolerance for the kinds of organizational loyalty they see acted out around them.

For instance, an older worker (thirty-five plus) may actually talk about how good the organization has been to him or how much the company cares about its people. The young worker is openly amused and then astonished that anyone could think an entity capable of caring about anything. In his or her opinion it's almost anthropomorphic. Even when the young express that viewpoint, however tentatively (an almost unknown quality in that age group anyway), the older worker sees it as a threat to the organization's existence. He or she sees the younger person as saying that the organization doesn't care. The worker who's spent thirty years of his or her life and a great deal of emotional energy liking or even loving the organizational entity has been kidding himself or herself—the modern enactment of the fable of the emperor's new clothes. As you recall, the emperor was conned into going naked through the streets on the theory that the clothes he wore were so fine that only he could see them. It

was a child who finally said what others hardly dared think—
that the emperor was nude. It could hardly be more politically
inept for the younger worker to reenact that scene. We don't
know whether the child in the fable was beheaded—but if he or
she had been between eighteen and twenty-four, it would have
been a possibility.

Young workers don't see themselves as having to pay their
political dues. They tend to see skills—the physical or intellectual ability to do the job—as all-important. Since the education
system ill prepared them for the politics of the work environment, they are sure the reason they don't advance the first few
weeks is because the organization values seniority and doesn't
want new ideas. Putting aside the argument of seniority versus
ability, the one kind of knowledge that it takes time to acquire is
a knowledge of office politics.

You'll never get a course on practical politics in either under-
graduate or graduate business school. In the first place, business
schools don't like processes as troublesome and untidy as office
politics. Second, until you've really been in an organization with
something at stake (such as your job), you've had no incentive
to learn the rules and curb your righteous, judgmental impulses.

It's just the same as teaching sex through movies and just as
experiential. Paying your dues doesn't mean that you have to
kowtow or compromise your values—just that you don't take a
stand based on zero knowledge, defending it until your career
goes up in flames.

Richard Nelson Bolles reports in *What Color Is Your Parachute?* that workers under thirty-five change jobs on the average
of every eighteen months, those over thirty-five on the average
of every three years. It's likely that some of these young workers
made serious political errors. They may have left jobs feetfirst.

In our research the most common errors young employees
made were these:

1. *Expecting promotions on about the same schedule that
schools keep.*

One of the problems new workers have is that they think
promotions are time-linked. This is rare. All public and private
education is geared to a calendar year. If you're a sophomore
this year and you perform, you can expect to be a junior next
year. Promotions in business rarely occur this way because they

depend on selling someone on the idea of promoting you instead of being an automatic process. Promotions are often affected by the availability of openings—something even top management can't always predict or control. When you first get into the work arena, the neat structure of education is hard to give up. Most young workers don't even want to give it up. They prefer the automatic movement that the education system provided. Once you realize that it's not only entirely different in practice but also organized according to different assumptions, it's much easier to work at politics instead of just putting in time.

Even in government, job promotions are not as automatic as they were in educational systems. Here again, the problems of availability have an influence as well as the changing pressures on government to do different kinds of things.

2. *Subjecting every management decision to a test of rightness and fairness.*

The business of any organization, profit or nonprofit, is survival. Many decisions are based on the need to ensure the survival of the organization. The more education you have, the more you understand this intellectually—and the less likely you are to understand it at gut level. Even people with master's degrees in business administration from very impressive universities use the phrase *It's not fair* more than their educational background and presumed savvy would indicate they should.

The new worker does not come off as a sensitive, caring person—just politically naive. This behavior keys right into the belief of older workers that the young are ruined by too much education—that they're not street smart.

3. *Looking for the definitive answer and refusing to compromise short of total victory.*

The young aren't alone in this, but it's forgivable in them. It's just plain aggravating in older workers who should know better. There are so few total victories in organizations that it's worthwhile reading the business sections of newspapers and the business press just to know when and where they occur.

In the first place, when a big decision has to be made, the issues are rarely perfectly clear. Second, there's saving face, which really means not letting anyone lose so completely that he or she has to leave the organization in disgrace. That would threaten the continued life of the organization and is very important to top management. They put the organization's survival before anything else. Wanting to "win big" is a threat to organizational survival because someone or many people have to lose big. The emotional appeal of the big win—the contract that saves the business, the decision that turns things around, the insight that clarifies the issue for everybody—is irresistible. That's what the new worker wants. This is probably why older managers so often find new M.B.A.s from "good" schools intolerable. The young are looking for the clear, the definitive, the parting of the Red Sea.

Nothing but living inside an organization for a year or so will convince the younger worker that the nature of the organization discourages the big win. It won't be an easy idea to give up because, like an aspiring movie star, you might just do it. Still, what you can do as a new worker is not to talk about the big win or the corporate coup with people who will hold it against you politically. This strikes many young workers as hypocritical. Total honesty is not always the most judicious policy. Think of it as not revealing your hand in a poker game.

4. *Thinking that the need to gather voices on everything from what to serve at the organization's Christmas party to the kind of water cooler to install is hopeless indecisiveness on the part of top management.*

The constant brokering of decisions does not fit the decision models learned in school. The least we've come to expect of a decision is that it be recognizable as a decision with an originator. It takes young workers some time to realize that the constant input into the decision-making process from different kinds of people is not indecision on the part of management but selling. Top management can command only so much—then selling takes over. If you think about the thousands of ways workers can sabotage an organization by doing, or not doing, something, it's almost a miracle that any organization survives. As a result, management looks not just for tacit assent from the people in the organization but also for enthusiasm, some kind of emotional commitment. Especially in nonprofit organizations, which have less money to motivate people, management will try to sell decisions because they'll get more effort for the dollar (known as "more bang for the buck").

What managers have learned is that if you seem to have some

input into the decision, if you get to say what you'd like to see happen, they've sold you a piece of that decision. In theory at least, you'll work harder to make it happen since part of it "belongs" to you. Although this muddies the lines of responsibility, managers feel that it gets a better effort out of the troops.

For the young worker it's a slow-moving, cumbersome way to do things. Even case-study courses in college, during which the participants broker decisions among themselves, are inadequate preparation for the way organizations really make decisions. As with every political situation we've described, there are the more ponderous organizations and the less ponderous ones. Still, those that are fast and decisive are small in size—fewer people to consider—and not many of them exist.

5. *Letting the cruelty of some decisions and the cannibalization of some people perceived as innocent have a lasting effect on themselves.*

For instance, Michael, a person whose performance appraisals had been good, was fired in the following way. Michael remembers it well, as do all those in his department.

At 4:30 on Friday afternoon, just before the Christmas party at which annual bonuses were distributed, Michael was called into the boss's office. The boss said, "Do you remember six months ago I told you that things might not turn out around here? Well, they haven't. You're fired, effective immediately. Don't return to your office. Just go down to personnel, and they'll take care of you. We'll arrange to go through your office and separate what belongs to us from what belongs to you, and we'll pack it and have it shipped to your house. Good-bye." Michael stumbled out of his boss's office, was handed his coat by the boss's secretary, and went to personnel.

The effect on the rest of the people in the office was catastrophic. The most naive manager in the world should have expected that Michael could not disappear after having worked there for three years without some of his colleagues noticing and calling him at home to find out where he'd gone. When they heard the recital of events from the victim, they were appalled.

Within a few months most of the younger ones—still wrapped in some of their youthful idealism—had applied for transfers from the department or left the organization. The rest swallowed their anger and concentrated on doing their jobs and avoiding the boss. The way his subordinates isolated the boss was almost tangible. You could practically see the space bubble that separated him from the troops. Eventually, management above the boss worked his job description over, promoted some of his subordinates, put other people in layers around him, and diffused his power. They reorganized the department around his still warm body. They did not fire him, though every person in the department might have prayed for that every night.

That's really the point from the younger worker's point of view. Cruelty isn't dealt with in kind. There is nothing to suggest that the boss even associated his political decline with the firing of his subordinate. The story, as can be imagined, was repeated throughout the organization. Each one of 1,650 employees heard it. The younger the worker, the more extreme the reaction and sense of outrage. The older workers just shrugged. They weren't even particularly surprised. No one from that department failed to go over every ugly detail at his or her exit interview.

No one would suggest that you have to like, accept, or condone that sort of behavior on the part of the people for whom you work. Keep in mind that every decision made by a manager is not necessarily in agreement with his or her boss's wishes or expectations. Many other people in the organization would not have fired Michael as his boss did. To judge the organization solely on the basis of one incident—as so many of the younger people who heard about it did—is neither accurate nor realistic.

WORKERS OVER FORTY

Until recently the most horrible stories that circulated among job hunters concerned the specter of being fired in one's fifties. This was seen as justification for any behavior—even suicide.

People over forty were easy prey for fast-buck con artists who offered jobs. Each person over forty could recite at length the travail of someone he or she knew who'd been fired and hadn't gotten a job for years. Personnel people would admit, after a few scotches, that they were inclined not to hire people over fifty except at very high levels.

What happened to change this picture is the change in the retirement law. The law made mandatory retirement at age sixty-five illegal, with certain exceptions. Many companies had been willing to keep a worker in his or her forties—even though he or she had ceased to be productive—when the organization could retire the worker at fifty-five. This was known as "taking early retirement." With the change in the retirement law such that most organizations cannot force determined employees to retire before seventy, there has been a massive reevaluation vis-à-vis the older worker. Many people who had it made and were really coasting have been awakened by more stringent performance appraisals, more insistence from their bosses on increased output, and even direct threats of firing. The result has been much more movement between jobs of people in the over-forty and over-fifty age groups. Instead of the fear that they will be fired and never get another job, older workers have a whole new set of worries.

The politics of being over forty tends to be the politics of the staying action. How can I get the organization to keep me around as long as I'd like to stay without having to work as hard as I did in my twenties and thirties? In other words, how can I coast without losing my job? If this is your ambition, you'll have to play defensive politics. As the economy moves both up and down, there will be problems with purely defensive politics. If the economy declines, you'll have to be vastly more productive. As it improves, you'll be able to coast somewhat. This is not to suggest that all workers in their forties and fifties want to coast and are uninterested in advancement. On the contrary, some are still climbing the mountain in high gear. However, a great many want to hold on rather than advance. For them, the new law poses a threat.

Older workers surrounded by older workers have more of an opportunity to succeed with a coasting strategy than do those who are surrounded by the young—especially the under-thirty crowd. Many of these younger workers see their only road to advancement as bumping off an older worker, thereby creating an opening. The more young workers surround the older worker, the more competitive the atmosphere. In fact, the mix of ages breeds more competition to produce than that among workers all of the same age. As an organization becomes all of any one thing—all one age, all one sex, all one kind of background— some of the yeast that leavened the organization diminishes.

With everybody thinking about things in the same way, it's much easier to cooperate rather than compete.

There will always be some conflict between older and younger workers. A boss in his or her fifties will feel more comfortable with workers not more than ten to fifteen years younger. The boss will feel that he or she is running a day nursery if surrounded by people in their twenties. As a result, the boss may seek more contact with the older workers—those nearer his or her age—at the expense of the younger workers. The younger ones will see this as the forming of an exclusive group, and attitudes will harden along age lines. This fathers a further problem because it cuts the manager off from the younger workers and their internal networks. The manager is much less likely to be able to control the flow of information when he or she doesn't hear things until they're practically in print in the company newsletter.

The older worker needs to keep his or her contacts both within and outside of the organization. Unless he or she does this, the sense of job insecurity—especially in those organizations that pride themselves on being youthful—will be overwhelming. Any worker over forty who finds himself or herself suddenly reporting to a boss five to ten years younger will be glad to have kept up with his or her contacts. Then if the older worker decides, for whatever reason, that he or she has had enough of the situation, the possibilities to move, without the humiliation of going through personnel, are far greater.

All of the workers we've talked about in this chapter have both a great need and a great incentive to take an active role in office politics. Unless they plug into the internal networks and get as much information as possible, they run two risks: isolation and possible job failure, and faulty diagnosis of the situations to the extent that they react in the wrong way. Many of Elizabeth's problems were age-related. As were Harry's. Both could have done better in their respective job situations had they had better information. That, of course, is what this book is about.

Chapter 9

The Nature
of Nonprofits—
or Doing Good
Can Be Disastrous

Harry's first job left him bitterly disillusioned. He felt so
strongly that he'd been mistreated that he decided he'd never
work for a capitalist again if he could help it. He looked around
at the nonprofit organizations in his area and chose a social
service agency. The office politics couldn't be as bad in an organization dedicated to helping people, he decided.

At first everything seemed ideal. He was helping people get
essential services—food stamps—and he felt some satisfaction
in this. One day his boss asked him if he really believed in what
he was doing. Harry was confounded. Would he be working
there if he didn't believe the work both important and worthwhile?

"Yes," his boss said, "but I don't get the feeling that you're
really committed at gut level. I'm not sure you really believe
people should get food stamps." Harry choked out an appropriate response.

Harry called Elizabeth, and they met for a drink. Both were
surprised that Harry's boss wasn't satisfied. What did the boss
really want? Harry's performance was well above that turned in
by his peers. But the boss seemed to like them better. Back to
politics.

In theory, the internal politics of nonprofit organizations and businesses should be pretty much the same. After all, they are organized along the same hierarchical lines. The same kinds of people appear to manage and work for them. The same skills and educational backgrounds are required for similar jobs in both. Other than the names used to describe the jobs, the genuine differences should be small. This is a serious misconception.

Two startling but inescapable facts emerged from our research into the politics of nonprofit organizations. First, the worker has a far better chance of being a political victim because of the assumptions nonprofits make about themselves, their missions, and their organizational structures. Second, the process of office politics takes up much more time in nonprofits; it's used more destructively, if more creatively, and the rules are different.

The assumptions that both managers and workers make about the nonprofit and the way it should work override every other consideration and color every activity. The myth that runs through all nonprofits—schools, trade and professional associations, universities, hospitals, government units, and social service agencies—is that the people who work for them are trading the extra dollars they could command from the same or similar jobs in industry for job security.

Government workers feel the civil service exists to protect their jobs. Teachers feel secure with tenure. Other people are certain that if they are sacrificing to work for a *charitable* institution, that institution wouldn't have the gall to let them go. It's not part of the rules of the game.

This myth is held at an emotional as well as at a rational level, and facts don't intrude. Because of the declining birthrate, school districts in many areas are forced to close schools. Any public schoolteacher can recognize that it's not possible to educate children who have not been born. That's logical. Thinking reasonably, if there are not enough children to fill a school, the school will close and the teachers will lose their jobs. At an emotional level, teachers are outraged by this. There has been a breach of the unspoken contract that existed between teacher and school board—at least on the teacher's side.

Tenure really isn't the issue. In the end, those with tenure will be unemployed if the cuts go deep enough. They call it RIF in some school districts, reduction in force. Tenured people may go later than the untenured ones, but they too will eventually be out of jobs. What's been interesting about the shrinking school-district populations has been the strikes or protests organized by teachers.

These occur to protest the cuts school boards have made or simply to let the community at large know how teachers feel. The strikes reflect the overwhelming anger and bitterness teachers feel at what they see as the unfairness of the loss of their jobs.

That anger and bitterness isn't directed at the parents who've failed to have enough children. It doesn't single out the deliberately childless couples, though both groups have caused the problem. It's an irrational striking out. School boards are just an incidental target. The boards are reacting to real conditions, budget cuts, and massive sociological change. No rational person can believe that a school board will operate the same number of schools, with the same number of teachers, for fifty thousand children as for a hundred thousand. In some areas the drop in school-age children has been that great or greater.

At gut level, teachers see a breach of the nonverbal contract between them and the school boards. Nobody ever mentions productivity in these discussions; people speak of following the rules or the procedures. As long as the teachers did what they were being paid to do, they had absolute job security once they were tenured. Tenure was supposed to protect jobs, not academic freedom. Once teachers had paid their dues, been through the red tape of getting tenured, kept going to summer school, filled out all the forms, attended the endless meetings, and followed the ever-changing rules and curricula, the job was supposed to be there. The teachers were supposed to have jobs as long as they wanted to teach, right up to retirement.

Absolute job security was the basic assumption teachers had about their jobs. "I don't make as much money as I'd make in industry, but I don't have to worry about being fired either" was the rallying cry. Realizing bitterly that tenure is useless and job security a myth, many people are leaving teaching voluntarily, even though their jobs are quite secure.

This is a far less idealistic explanation than the one offered by teachers. Their protests are organized to "make the community aware of the quality of education," or because they're "worried about the children." In fact, job security is the issue.

If you carefully research hospitals, social service agencies, universities, trade and professional associations, and government, you will find that same underlying assumption on the part of both worker and management. Management's assumption is that "We're paying people less because we promise that their jobs are secure." It's a trade-off of fewer dollars for lower risk. The workers who choose these jobs embrace this concept most eagerly.

Of course, there are also businesses that seem to offer absolute job security. "We never get rid of anybody. We're just one big, happy family," you'll hear. (You'll hear it from management; rarely from the workers.) Businesses with aggressive paternalism tend to be family owned; they also tend to be smaller businesses. General Motors doesn't make that sort of commitment publicly.

Still, most people realize that if the business got into trouble, it would lay off employees. That would be prudent and businesslike—really the only sensible course of action. The fact is that there is no absolute job security in any kind of organization, nonprofit or business. The myth lives because people want to believe it, and it's a killer. Otherwise sensible people behave irrationally in that one area. They act as if wishing or pretending that job security were absolute could make it so.

As we've seen before, mistaking myth for fact tends to profoundly affect organizational politics. Budget cuts, political changes, and reorganizations hit all kinds of organizations. Still, facts have never dented a myth that people want to believe as badly as they do the myth of absolute job security.

Unless you understand this myth, you can't begin to understand the politics of nonprofit organizations. It means that the people who choose careers in nonprofits or who choose to practice their skills in a nonprofit environment do so deliberately. It's a deliberate turning away from the profit sector. They have made certain assumptions about the nature of nonprofits. They believe nonprofits meet more of their needs and expectations. You cannot understand the political environment in any nonprofit organization unless you examine the assumptions those working in the organization have made. If you are thinking of a job in a nonprofit, it's important to examine the political environment and learn the rules that govern it.

All nonprofits exist to provide some kind of service to a particular public. No one nonprofit, even the federal government, provides a single service to everyone. In fact, the federal government is subdivided into different groups producing different services for different publics.

The underlying assumptions about the service provided are: (1) it's something the client group needs and that is important; (2) it's something only a nonprofit can provide—businesses either can't or won't; and (3) it's going to make the lives of the clients better, richer, safer, saner, and so on, in the long run. (Yes, even the Internal Revenue Service sees its role in that light.)

This sense of holy mission may diminish over the years as the nonprofit ages or changes. It may seem to be lost entirely. It may be ridiculed by many of the people who are supposed to be committed to that mission. It may be denied outright—but it does exist as an underlying assumption. Otherwise there would have been no reason to organize the activity as a nonprofit.

MANAGEMENT ASSUMPTIONS

At this point the assumptions of the managers of nonprofits diverge from those of the people they manage, just as they sometimes do in business. The assumptions both groups make are so important, however, that we must look carefully at them before we can understand the internal politics.

Both managers and workers assume that nonprofits do not have, and never can have, enough money to do all that needs to be done. It's not a question of making or raising more money; it's simply not possible to get enough money to run the organization as it should be run. They see themselves as perpetually underbudgeted, living in the shadow of financial failure. There will always be a smaller economic pie to cut up than in a business of the same size, they believe. As a result, managers assume that they should not have to pay as much for things as businesses do. That way their paltry funds will stretch farther. This idea is encouraged by their tax-exempt status and the many discounts and special deals that businesses offer nonprofits.

It is more visible in the assumption by management that they should not have to pay as much for workers at any level as they would have to pay if they managed a business. The assumption that they can get the same quality employee for less money than a business would have to pay, because the nonprofit's cause is just and people should want to work for the cause, leads to a fairly constant disappointment. Should they manage to find a high performer for a bargain, that person tends to move on once he or she realizes no more money is in the wings.

Universities talk of their "intellectual atmosphere" and "academic environment." These are selling points, an intangible compensation. Hospitals push their lifesaving mission. Trade and professional associations speak of "service to the profession" and its members, and the government waves the flag.

Managers may try to trade a lower salary and slower advancement based heavily on seniority for the worker's missionary zeal, prestige needs, or overwhelming desire to be part of a "good" organization.

This lower pay scale is no secret to workers. What they think—and it's what makes teachers so angry—is that they are giving up a higher, market-level pay scale for absolute, or almost absolute, job security. That is why they see layoffs and firings as a breach of the basic employment contract. Firing for cause is as much a breach of this contract as are budget layoffs. Many teachers say flat out that they would never have chosen teaching had they not expected that, once tenured, they would never have to push again. They had expected to reach a plateau and rest there.

University professors feel equally outraged when departments are closed and they are let go. It's not just the teachers but staff as well who experience this outrage. Many staff people feel they have, or ought to have, tenure, too.

Every time a teacher is laid off, a shudder goes through the staff that knew or heard about that victim. The interest in and commitment to job security is absolute. As one woman at a major university in Philadelphia said, "I can't wait to get out of here. My job's not on the line, and my department is in great shape. But the people here have completely shut down. They know only one issue, one topic, one hot button, and that's whether there will be more layoffs and, if so, when. Nobody has done, or is going to do, a bit of work until the job situation stabilizes. I don't want to be here as things get worse even though I will have a job. I don't know a colleague, staff or faculty, who would hesitate to stab his or her mother to keep the job—and they aren't really very good jobs! The politics is brutal because, if someone's forced out, there may be an opening. At least someone won't get laid off."

Trade and professional associations cannot sell security to the degree the other nonprofits have because they are subject to enormous member and officer pressures. Still, their people seem to have much the same attitude as did those in educational institutions.

Job security doesn't just mean layoffs, as in the case of teachers or an agency's closing for lack of funding. It covers dismissals for cause as well. There is a reluctance in most nonprofits to dismiss even the aggressive nonperformer if the person has been there a long time, say, ten years or more. This can be carried to such extremes that it jeopardizes the survival of the nonprofit and everybody else's job.

For example, an agency had an employee in a critical staff function who was an acute alcoholic. The man had been unable to do his job or manage his four-person staff for ten of the twenty-five years he'd been at the agency. He was in charge of audiovisual materials and the scheduling of the use of videotape recorders and training films.

Ten years ago the agency's use of videotape to train employees and clients and as an important part of the educational process had been minimal. For the past five years, agency trainers had used the equipment daily.

The department manager's loss of memory, slowness, long absences from work, and general inefficiency drove the trainers wild. They complained vociferously to the head of the agency. His response was that the man had been with the agency for twenty-five years and that if the director fired him, he'd probably end up a bum on skid row.

As a result of this humane decision, the agency continued to sacrifice the interests of its 6,500 clients and forty-five staff members in the name of institutional loyalty to one man. At the time the problem heated up, the man was forty-eight—some seventeen years from retirement.

Many of the staff, tired of a hopeless hassle and no sign of change, either gave up or moved on as opportunities presented themselves. The quality of training remained at a low level. The alcoholic remained. What is remarkable about this case—there are thousands like it—was that the agency head refused to insist that the man get help at the price of his job. His rationale was that forcing the man to get help would push him to quit and "be a bum full time."

The stories about universities that keep senile, criminally bewildered, or deranged professors in the classroom and on the payroll because they are tenured and it's too much trouble to remove them are legion. Associations keep executive directors who are too senile to make good house pets, much less administrators, out of a kind of nostalgia. As in the case of the alcoholic worker, our interest is not in the fact that this goes on but in the effect it has on the organization's politics.

Workers seem to understand two things about top management in nonprofits: (1) Managers don't have to be sensible and businesslike. There is often no reason for what is done except a vague principle that even top management can't explain, for example, "He'll end up on skid row." And, (2) logical argument has even less importance than in business when it comes into conflict with a moral or quasi- or pseudomoral principle.

For instance, if an accounting clerk at an agency continues to make mistakes until the financial health of the agency is in danger—if anyone could get the records together enough to find out what was happening—top management might or might not fire him or her. They might not even insist that his or her performance within a definite period improve. In a business, such a threat to the organization's survival would be dealt with pronto.

Other workers, watching the accounting clerk sink the ship, are moved to greater resentment, not greater productivity. The ones who have seniority similar to the clerk's see a similar immunity from the ordinary penalties of incompetence and nonperformance. Productive workers get tired of carrying the loser or tired of trying to figure out why no one else cares. Either they get on with their work, having deadened any sense of responsibility to the management, fellow workers, or the institution as a whole, or they leave.

Management has fairly low expectations about its people: "We don't pay them anything, so what can we expect?" A fascinating study might be an analysis of the accuracy of management's expectations. Are people attracted to nonprofits by the prospect of doing nothing for a small salary? Do they lower their own performance standards when they see that no rewards are available for outstanding productivity? Do they come to the nonprofit with higher or more humane standards?

What is prudent and rational in business is seen as "cold-blooded" and "lacking social conscience" in nonprofits. Politically this means that every argument for or against an issue or idea must anticipate this obsession and be coated in a socially correct veneer.

Having to treat the purchase of paper and string as a moral issue defeats many employees. The rest torture every argument to make it fit the accepted moral configuration. It's not big moral issues that worry nonprofits. It's not the South Africas and defensive wars. It's rampant moral freebies. Is it proper for us to serve ordinary white sugar with coffee, or are we contributing to people's decline? Are those of us who bicycle to work while wearing vasectomy pins inherently more valuable to the agency because of our life-styles? Are those of us who take colicky infants to the office and breast-feed them with the ostentation of the Pharisees praying in the Temple courtyard setting an example for the great unwashed?

One of the more powerful negatives in the relationships between managers and employees is that people at very low levels become more powerful than their bosses. A secretary to the dean of a liberal arts college remains while the dean rotates every six to nine years. She has more power because she is a given, a part of the furniture. The dean has to win her acceptance—not the other way around. She holds many information keys that the dean needs. She is tied into many internal networks. Her views may become the dean's views unless he has other internal sources he can tap. In theory, a new executive should be able to name his or her own secretary. In many nonprofits, the secretary comes with the job.

Managers who are unable to dismiss the incompetent and willful nonperformer have few options to spur performance from the troops. Since the employee cannot be fired unless he or she steals, acts against the nonprofit's values (a Catholic in a Catholic institution who had an abortion and let this be known could expect management to find a way to dump her), or causes a serious problem with the clientele that threatens the nonprofit's survival or reputation, he or she is relatively worry-free. Simple goldbricking or incompetence will rarely result in dismissal. In fact, if someone were dismissed for nonperformance, it would start an emotional landslide.

This leaves the manager with only political weapons instead of organizational tools. As a result, political torture is far more common in nonprofits. It's the only tool management has.

A social worker rocks the boat and tells others about his dissatisfaction. His case load is rearranged. Instead of a manageable load in a fairly concentrated area, he's assigned cases randomly all over the city. His performance is questioned during a general staff meeting. His expense account must be accompanied by parking meter receipts and subway vouchers.

A university professor will suddenly learn that her chairman has changed the teaching schedule. The professor now teaches an eight o'clock class five mornings a week and a four o'clock class five afternoons a week. She's also assigned a nine-to-twelve class on Saturdays. The professor's tests get typed last; her photocopies are faint to the point of unreadability; her office is shared by the janitorial staff, which uses it as a broom closet at night; and colleagues, seeing her fall from grace, avert their eyes when she's around. Political Siberia might be catching. This treatment will rarely, however, cause the professor to leave. She'll just be miserable.

The same sort of games go on in public and private schools. The teaching load is increased to a killing level. Help is unavailable. Every mistake the employee makes is picked up, picked at, and passed around to other employees. Managers in nonprofits know how to use the internal information networks when they want to, and most use them vindictively.

In associations, the staff member is assigned to wet-nurse the most boring, mindless, and demanding of the association's officers. This means providing personal services, such as making hair appointments, making restaurant reservations, choosing gifts for family and friends, and personally picking up show tickets across town. The staff member is sent on the road at inconvenient times to deal with the most disagreeable members and chapters. The executive director begins to undermine the staff member's work, asking his or her peers if they think the target is really able to perform. This plants the seed in everybody's mind that the answer is no. The target is made aware that all this is going on.

There are closed-door meetings, or people arrive early and stay until after the victim has left. Ultimately, the target is sentenced to have some of the members and staff for dinner at his or her house. Julia Child refuses to cater. Still, the staff person may not leave.

In every case the manager's ultimate weapon is isolation. This technique may get the unwanted one to leave even if he or she has been clinging like a label to a mayonnaise jar. The target is cut off from, and out of, as many internal networks as possible. Other employees go along. The healthier the target's ego, the sooner he or she will leave. If the target decides to stick it out, he or she may continue to collect a salary and do nothing.

There is less employee independence from management because employees, obsessed with their own job security, feel threatened. If management lets it be known that the target is about to be axed, even if the other employees know that this is impossible or at least very difficult, the troops will tend to avoid the target. They are afraid, at gut level, that this falling from grace might be extended to them.

You've undoubtedly observed by now that the political environment in nonprofits, nurtured by management's real helplessness in keeping the troops working and inability to clear up past hiring mistakes by firing, produces viciousness of a very refined sort. It colors the political environment and makes vital differences in the ways employees work with each other and with management.

Of course, businesses also use terror as a weapon against employees. The difference is that no business manager can afford to play over a period of years. He or she can fire people and will. In fact, managers who never fire are often seen as weak! Some companies, unable to bear the harshness of outright dismissal, use outplacement. Outplacement specialists are corporate undertakers who remove the loser's still warm body without making management feel guilty. They help the victim find a new job.

Further misleading the employees of nonprofits is the "We're all one happy family here" myth. The idea is that we don't just work here—we're emotionally committed to what we do and the people we do it with and for. This leads many people to think that there is no office politics because people all genuinely like each other. They are wrong. As we've said, there is no organization of human beings working together free of political push and shove. Families are highly political, as anyone who's ever been executor of a will and had to deal with the heirs can tell you!

The "We're all one happy family" myth encourages workers to believe that, unlike those money-grubbing business people, their bosses know them and care about them on an individual level. They want to believe—many genuinely do—that their bosses are far more personally involved in the workers' needs and aspirations than would be the case in a business concerned with profit and loss. Many workers see this caring as an essential part of the politics of the organization. They also believe that their bosses feel this way because they are more altruistic than managers in businesses, not because it is in the manager's best interests to convince the troops he or she feels that way.

Since managers in nonprofits are well aware that genuine caring is an important worker expectation, they at least act out this role. Because workers are expecting to be evaluated on a more personal level than a strictly professional one, the worker naturally personalizes each shred of criticism. There is no distancing here. Workers are frequently very upset when told to change behaviors that they might expect to be overlooked by a true friend or family member. They don't expect to be evaluated as rigorously as they would be in businesses for all the reasons we've discussed. "Look, if I'm going to have to work as hard and produce as much here as I would if I worked for a business, why am I here?" one man asked.

Although managers in nonprofits talk about professionalism, their words have less effect. The combination of lower salary and family aura defeats what is said. The manager's ability to be "understanding" and "forgiving" of employee nonperformance is always limited by two things: (1) his or her personal understanding of the institution's limits of tolerance and (2) his or her own personal limits of tolerance. In the end, there is bound to be resentment and frustration on both sides. This has a major effect on the political environment.

The idea of family benefits management as well as makes things difficult. Since there is usually little question of management paying workers for overtime, the family metaphor helps get employees to "pitch in for the good of the group." This may be talked about very sincerely on both sides, but it is a political artifice useful in trying to get extra effort out of the workers. Again this technique may be tried in businesses, but eventually the employees are going to shout for more money and vote with their feet.

Closely tied to the family idea is the idea that each employee must make an emotional commitment to whatever cause the nonprofit serves. As Harry discovered, it's not enough to perform competently, even outstandingly. The emotional commitment must be there, it must be expressed, and it must be expressed frequently. Associations are especially demanding in this respect. The executive director must receive continued assurance that staff members are committed at an emotional level to the goals and aims of the association. This can sometimes be carried to such absurdity that staff people are expected not just to respond positively but also to think up examples of why they are heart and soul in favor of that association.

Part of this is probably a need to keep the volunteer members jacked up. Part of it, however, is a way of controlling staff members and the political environment. Unless there is an emotional commitment to the association, staff members may think in terms of change. They may see flaws in the structures that clients or members must believe in fervently in order to support and use the association and its services. By putting emotional commitment into the employee equation, the employee is less likely to express criticism of the staff director, the organization's goals, or the performance of members. In associations, loyalty is measured by the degree of emotional commitment.

Another reason for the demand for emotional commitment is that it helps bind the better staff people to the organization. Since money can't be offered to buy loyalty, nonprofits try to get loyalty by screening up front for emotional commitment.

There is no panacea for improving employee retention, but it's fairly clear that neither buying loyalty nor screening out the people who aren't likely to be loyal gets the job done. In the end, trade and professional associations probably have the highest turnover of all nonprofits .

The emphasis on attitude and feeling, especially in associations and social service agencies, sets up a situation in which the nonproductive employee can turn the tables. He or she can defend poor performance with examples of his or her superior emotional commitment and attitude. The willingness of enough managers to overlook poor performance for good attitude, however the latter is defined, keeps people polishing attitudes at the expense of performance. Nonprofit organizations represent the final, the absolute triumph of form over substance, of work style over productivity.

A trade association ran an education program of questionable quality for its members. A few of the brighter officers began to complain to the executive director, questioning the competence of the educational director. The executive director talked about the educational director's fine relationships with members, her fine image, and her length of service with the association. Valid questions and complaints were ignored or pooh-poohed, and the issue became the members' and officers' lack of appreciation. "Our educational director has just the image we need," the executive director said.

Because the range of acceptable staff attitudes is constricted, any one employee's range of responses is restricted. Since every remark, fact, or opinion will be given a loyalty test before it's considered, employees tend to be careful about what they say. This has a major impact on any employee's willingness and ability to point out problems—even very large ones. To suggest that the association's training programs were far inferior to the sort that any business would tolerate and that they should, and could, be improved would be an act not of businesslike, prudent behavior but of disloyalty.

The emotional investment in those training programs may approach the fervor of a parent for a new infant, and criticism be received as gladly. By asking employees to invest emotionally in every aspect of the nonprofit's activities, all change becomes two or three times as difficult. The risk to the staff member who points out flaws or suggests improvements is enormous. Those who discover the need for change and the reluctance to accept that need try once or twice; then they move on.

The political cost of this is to put a premium on method acting and hypocrisy. While businesses have individual managers who encourage this kind of thing, the business as a business could not officially agree with or encourage this kind of behavior. In nonprofits it comes with the territory. The problem is that each employee has to decide where he or she draws the line between candor and truth. Given the family aura, the loyalty issue, and the need to be mutually supportive, truth is far down the list of priorities.

Universities, public schools, and hospitals have a greater tolerance for unvarnished truth than have trade and professional associations and agencies. The former are operating under the more or less continuous scrutiny of the public and press. They can expect lots of trouble from any attempt to cover up the facts or to misrepresent them. That doesn't mean people in these institutions don't try. It's just more difficult.

The family aura tends to give the staff of associations and social service agencies a feeling of us, the staff, versus them, the clients. We the staff are plagued with this incompetent group of clients, members, or taxpayers. We are so much cleverer, better educated, and morally straighter than the people we serve. There is a love/hate side to every client relationship, but the level of contempt expressed by the staff for the people it serves far exceeds that expressed in a business/client relationship. Surely, the people in advertising agencies are capable of cutting up an obnoxious client. They generally have good verbal skills and some wit. There is, however, a tendency to treat such behavior as highly unprofessional in large agencies—simply something that is not done. Big agencies frown on expressions of contempt for the bill payers. Not so in nonprofits!

The ways in which the staffs of trade and professional associations and social service agencies excel at making fun of the foibles and excesses of the client group (behind their backs, of course) is unbelievable. No advertising agency president could spend the time making fun of his or her clients or swapping stories with his or her underlings that association executive directors and staff people do. This has a very strong effect on the internal political environment. It does not breed solidarity among the staff. Instead, it breeds a strong distrust among staff members because each suspects that the other's remarks are not always limited to the clients.

This tends to be especially true in single-sex associations or agencies served by a single-sex staff. It would be difficult to tell whether men are more vicious about men, or women about women. When a mixed staff serves a mixed membership, the level of pure meanness tends to go down simply because one sex doesn't want the other to know the full extent of its pettiness.

Government agencies can't seem to control the contempt the staff members exhibit for the client groups they serve face to face. The clients are rarely unaware of these attitudes, but the more they need the service, the more likely the client is to swallow the abuse without responding. This further increases the staff's sense of power over the client and contempt for the client's powerlessness. Without the power to discipline employees who aren't performing or who abuse the client group, the client's only recourse is guerrilla warfare against the agency. The new employee walking into such a situation would not know that his or her political problems were going to include the ability to withstand pressure from without and within.

All the characteristics we've described tend to obscure the most important difference between businesses and nonprofits. In nonprofits there is a much greater centralization of power. Nonprofits may make the same show as businesses of collecting the voices for decisions, but the fact is that all power is in one hand or a very few hands. This can produce two negatives: Either someone who cannot delegate the selection of rubber bands heads the group, or someone who can't decide how things should be done and rarely makes any decision is in charge. There are shades in between, but our research indicates that nonprofits tilt one way or the other. It's a reverse bell curve. Both extremes produce significant problems.

For instance, the executive director of an association had a staff of twenty professionals to run an association of twenty-five thousand members. The director handpicked each subordinate after having done everything but test the candidate's blood. Still, the director felt the need to screen each piece of work that went out of the staff office. Knowing that the membership of the association was far less educated and far more conservative than its staff members, the director was obsessed with the possible reaction of the members to each piece of correspondence.

By concentrating all power in one spot, the director could stall projects for months and bring the association's business to a complete halt at will. Just leaving town would throw work production off by weeks. The result was a political environment in which turnover was so high that the association members couldn't even keep track of the names of staff members as they moved through the office.

You can imagine how extreme the problems were because most association staff people hope to retire from the staff, not seek another job. The members were told that the director wanted only the best people for the staff and that the high turnover was a result of high expectations. They appeared mollified. But eventually more questions were raised about turnover. The members began demanding an explanation for the fact that staff directors turned over once a year. The director could hardly offer the explanation of an inability to delegate and a pathologically large ego. As usually happens, one staff member told the officers of the association privately what was going on. Eventually, the director was replaced, but not before the staff, apart from the director, had changed completely three times in six years.

In most associations and agencies, the turnover problem would not have disturbed the officers unless it reduced the level of service the officers expected. In the case we described, the membership was very conservative and saw the revolving door as a negative. It went against the grain.

The other extreme in nonprofit management is the entire abdication of power. The power that resides in a director is never delegated; it just oozes around like warm Jell-O. The director never directs but never delegates either. This makes every decision a group decision, raises the risk for others, and reduces the director's risk to zero. He or she absolutely refuses to have the last word. Nothing can be done unless all agree. The relative importance of the decision makes no difference in the way the decision is made. Whether it's to buy baby-blue coffee cups or to cut the staff in half, all decisions are put through the same ponderous procedure.

The net result of both the autocratic and the nonmanagerial style is to produce low staff productivity, high political activity, and a high degree of cynicism in many people watching the process—not least of all the client group.

All these aberrations produce political problems for people who move from business to nonprofit or from school directly to a nonprofit. The rule of checking references on a boss in business is doubly important in a nonprofit. If you make a mistake in choosing a nonprofit, you can be so sucked in by the party line that, if you fail there, you'll be convinced that you're incompetent or worse. You may not recognize it as a political, not a skills, failure. Since the emotional involvement is bound to be greater in this kind of organization, you'll want to review the material on personal distancing in chapter 2. Without that process you'll be an emotional wreck.

Keep in mind that nonprofits are rarely malevolent by design. Businesses have lots of ways of cannibalizing workers, too. The real differences, as we've seen, lie in the attitudes of top management and the way these become part of the personnel policies. You need this information unless you want to walk blithely into a nonprofit, expecting it to live up to its shining image. If you know what to expect, you can assess the risks to your sanity and career and make an informed choice.

trying to cheer up a group of productive but normally gloomy people. Unless their actions or their attitudes affect the bottom line, or their conflicts reduce productivity or increase turnover, leave the troops alone. The desire to "adjust" people, environments, even events, is always there. It's a temptation to make things better. Most people don't get into management jobs unless they have some desire to work through others and to control people and events, or at least to lead the parade in some way.

THE REALITY OF OFFICE POLITICS

The hardest ridge for most managers to climb is the other side of the ridge they stumbled on as workers: acknowledging the existence of office politics. There is always a reluctance to say publicly that office politics is a part of the life of every manager as well as of every worker.

Of course, you don't gallop to the public address system and say, "Attention, attention. Office politics is a part of all our working lives, and there's not a bloody thing you can do about it." That would be as bizarre as it would be entirely accurate and honest. For the manager, acknowledgment means no hypocrisy, no telling subordinates that everything that happens in the office can be measured by the golden rule. Many managers think their status and personal credibility rest on convincing subordinates that decisions are made with the wisdom of Solomon by those higher up the ladder—always without political considerations, of course.

Acknowledge the fact that you—as well as they—know that every business decision, from the kind of bottled water used to the company with which one does business, has political elements. Everything you do is not going to strike each subordinate as the wisdom of Solomon. You do, in fact, like some people better than others. You have both political friends and political enemies. You are not in complete control of the bizarre politics going on companywide.

Managers have a need to play God, to a greater or lesser degree, depending on the health of their egos. This is as much a fact of political life for subordinates as the color of the manager's eyes—and as unchanging. The problem is that, in an attempt to seem The Leader, many managers confuse leading with being a guru or more infallible than the pope. Nothing reassures the troops more than working for a manager who doesn't play these games and is realistic about the organization's internal politics.

Don't kid yourself that your subordinates respect you—or will respect you—because you appear wise and infallible. They may, in fact, not respect you at all. They may be pretending. If they do respect you, it is probably because they think you're competent. Failing that, they respect you because you are a mean person and can cause them lots of trouble if they act disrespectful. If you acknowledge that you don't always understand why things happen within the organization, they'll have more respect for your honesty. Only a hypocrite pretends that he or she is never surprised.

Most managers don't want the troops to know that they don't have perfect control over the work environment because managers are concerned about saving face. For instance, Carol, manager of the small-loans department, said that it was all right for one man to take a two-hour lunch. He'd had a family emergency. The personnel department, however, sticks to the rules and charges the man for one hour's vacation time. Carol can do nothing—she's powerless.

If the workers know in advance that the manager can be overruled higher up on almost everything, it will not be very important to the politics of the work group. Politically, managers should never promise anything absolutely. If there's a shadow of a doubt that you'll be able to deliver, the troops need to know. If anything, your honesty will increase their respect.

This honesty—very different from the style advocated by management textbooks—produces a sense of security in the troops and a trust of the manager that has a very positive effect on the work environment. One theme running through worker complaints against management is that managers appear to think their subordinates are not mentally or morally strong enough to be told the truth. When we researched politics in the work environment in a number of different organizations, we found that the least candid managers had the lowest rate of credibility. No matter what your boss tells you about any particular issue and the need to follow the company line, it is your neck on the line with your subordinates.

If your subordinates are seriously unhappy with you, they can and will let you know in one of several ways: (1) They can make your existence *so* miserable that you'll find another job; (2) they can make your existence miserable in ways that make you sound petty and green with envy when you complain; (3) they can sabotage productivity to the point that your boss will take action; and (4) they can do exactly what you say and no more, refusing to exercise the slightest bit of independent judgment.

While folklore warns that a subordinate who rats on his or her boss, regardless of the provocation, is most likely to suffer, our research does not show that this invariably happens. In fact, it's about fifty-fifty. Fifty percent of the time subordinates can sink a manager, and 50 percent of the time they can't. Don't forget that your subordinates are appraising your performance as a manager nonstop. You are only one person. There are more of them and more shades of opinion on your performance in your role.

Anne worked for a large, prestigious New York City advertising agency. Even by industry standards, her boss was more than ordinarily neurotic. He began to do things that so upset the other people in the marketing department that turnover began to rise as productivity ceased abruptly.

His activities ranged from returning acceptable work with the notation that it "doesn't have it" or "hasn't been thought through completely" and needed more "incubation time" to rejecting without explanation material that had already been approved. The final blow came, however, on the day an entire project previously approved was rejected two days before the deadline for a client presentation. The boss's charge was to "come up with something else even if you have to sleep here until you do it."

A hurried meeting was called out of the boss's hearing. It was agreed that something had to be done before top management got wind of it. To go to the client with nothing would have been unthinkable. It was a division of the firm's largest, and most important, client.

It was physically impossible even to type a new marketing proposal in two days—much less develop one. In desperation Anne decided to see her boss's boss. She had little hope for such a meeting. She doubted he'd do anything, but he was reputed to be tough-minded and fair.

She went to his office, got in to see him, and explained the situation. He listened and asked some questions. To his ever-lasting credit he did not ask what Anne thought of her present boss or get into any personality issues at all. He was concerned that the presentation would be a disaster and that the entire firm would suffer. He did not promise to do anything except "look into things."

Anne never knew what he said or did. The next morning her boss called her in and told her that there wasn't time to do a new proposal. A sigh of relief went up. Three months later her boss departed for an unlucky competitor.

What this means to the manager is that the lines of authority aren't absolute. Someone higher up than you is responsible, so that in sticky times your boss may listen to the troops and act on what he or she hears.

Your peers are also doing performance appraisals on you at all times. They see what you do; they feel the effects. They judge your effectiveness as a manager. It's hard to overestimate the effect on someone who can boost your career when one of your peers talks about you in either admiring tones or one damning with faint praise.

Most managers are so hard pressed to get the work out or the product produced that they forget that the troops are making decisions about what's to be done and how. Just as the manager makes judgments about them, they are making judgments about the management.

If these decisions conflict, there may be more disagreement than is necessary and more political activity than the manager would like. To control the political activity in your department, you must know what the pecking order is among the troops.

The need to see power relationships among your subordinates in the working unit is greater in times of crisis. While it's impor-tant anytime, it may be the key to keeping the people you need to do your job during any merger, acquisition, or reorganization. Keeping in mind that the subordinates you value would prob-ably be valued by other managers, within and outside the or-ganization, you must be able to control rumors and put positive information into the network. To do this, it would be useful to know who within your unit passes along information.

Much as managers would like to either eliminate or at least

control the petty bickering that goes on among subordinates, they can't. In some ways eliminating the bickering, no matter how desirable, seems to cut you off from an important tool in assessing how your subordinates relate. If you hope to control the information that your people hear and believe, you'll want to concentrate on identifying the people the troops believe.

You may be surprised. They're not the people you'd see as credible at all. This happens all the time in both businesses and nonprofit organizations. Management's idea of who's reliable rarely matches the ideas of the managed.

Unless you look actively at the power arrangements your subordinates have set up among themselves, you will not be able to use or influence internal networks effectively. Being able to use the internal networks as skillfully as you'd play a guitar is vital. If you lacked every other quality desirable in a manager but did that one thing, you'd probably survive and prosper. Realizing, as with any list of do's and don'ts, that most people will pick and choose what's most important to them, we put a great deal of emphasis on this concept.

CONTROLLING INFORMATION NETWORKS

Most managers see the informal information system as a divisive influence. "Gossip should be discouraged," they say. "I wish I could stop that kind of thing." It can't be done, so stop trying. Rather than trying to stamp out rumors and gossip, it's far more productive to use those internal networks to combat misinformation or damaging information with more productive news.

The only way to control the internal information networks within your working unit is to first identify them; second, find out what kind of rumors are circulating; and third, insert your own news at strategic spots. Either rebut with facts or suggest different interpretations of information already in the network. Don't try to suppress anything.

If you hear the troops agitating about a change in the lunch hour and you know that top management really hasn't decided what the policy will be, that bit of information needs to circulate. It will give the troops a fact to pass around, and it will buy time while the decision is being made.

It will also give the troops a chance to express their views.

Regardless of the company's ultimate decision, the fact that people had a chance to tell how they felt is important. As you are taking information out of the troops' network, you are putting edited versions of that information into top management's network. If no decision has been made about the lunch-hour policy, top management needs to know how the troops react. The fact that the troops have been listened to often defuses some of the tension that accompanies change.

Anytime a new fact gets into the system, it alters the communication that's already going around. In so doing, it tends to soften the line between people in favor of something and people against it.

The more threatened people feel and the more their jobs are on the line, the more finely attuned will the grapevine be to every nuance and suggestion. If you know that things are none too stable, it's important to let your subordinates know. You can let them know you are aware of their fears, concerns, and problems without either endorsing or denying them.

Too many managers simply ignore the gossip even when they realize it's likely to drive the fearful and the most employable right out of the organization. Don't play ostrich. You need those people. For every employee there is a point at which the pain in a particular work situation outweighs the rewards. The closer the situation gets to that point for the majority of your people, the more decisively you must act.

The manager may be the only stabilizing influence during a crisis. The troops look to you to make some sense out of the often senseless events swirling around them, threatening the department or work unit. For instance, a rumor begins to make the rounds that the company is a target for an unfriendly takeover. You, the manager of the public relations department, are most surprised. Not a hint of this has been in the newspapers, not a whisper at the local drinking spas. No one at the last Publicity Club meeting shared this rumor with you, though in the past you've heard many, many rumors there. Your surprise is total.

You are certain that your subordinates, particularly the ones who work on the company's employee newsletter, have also heard rumblings. They cross-pollinate with enough people to have had someone mention it. Because they see people both inside and outside the organization every day, they pick up every nuance.

You call one of the assistant editors into your office and ask what she's heard. She gives you a rundown on the information she's picked up. Most of it has come from unlikely, yet logical places. One source was the son of the financial vice-president of the takeover company. He mentioned this to his unisex hairdresser to explain why he looked so tense. The hairdresser's boyfriend had gone to school with a woman in accounting, to whom he'd passed the rumor.

The second (and for the public relations director) even more credible source was the cleaning woman who'd been in an elevator with two executives from the takeover company. This is a common source of leaks.

For some reason, many executives make the arrogant assumption that a cleaning woman or janitor either doesn't have ears or, if he or she can hear, probably can't make sense out of what's being said. Both assumptions are ridiculous. The cleaning staff is in an ideal spot to know more of what's going on than just about anybody—though many of them have no desire to get involved with any of the rumors that move through the organization.

As public relations manager, it's important for you to be prepared, if indeed the company is under siege. You go to see your boss, the president. He flatly denies that there is an unfriendly takeover in the offing. He tells you to deny officially and privately that any takeover is possible, much less likely. Your own subordinates welcome you back from the president's office eager to know what's afoot. As manager, your first loyalty must be to the president—your own boss.

Still, if you believe the rumors are true, your own people are not going to respect you if you vehemently deny something that shortly turns out to be fact. You report only that the president said, "There are no unfriendly takeover attempts at this time." You do not endorse this view; you simply report it.

So many managers want to be in control of situations outside their control. Your subordinates encourage this. They want to believe that you, their manager, have a crystal ball. They want to believe that nothing bad will happen and that change will always be good. It can kill you politically with everybody to offer this kind of assurance. Resist the temptation. The president of the company can't guarantee a change-free environment. You'd have to be suicidal to try.

The control of information always involves risk. You can measure the level of risk as explained in chapter 3. Only take risks up to the level of your personal comfort. In our example, the manager transmits information without endorsing it. That's important, particularly during a crisis. Make this clear to your subordinates, or they will think that you are passing on to them a consensus with which you agree.

In our research, credibility rested on the manager's clear distinction—obvious to the troops—between what he or she believed to be true and the official view. Your superiors make this distinction in what they tell you, though they might deny it officially.

You will never have perfect control over the internal networks in your work unit. It will take a lot of trial and error to identify the people with whom it's most effective to place information. Sometimes the troops will refuse to repeat the information you've put into the network. If that happens, put the same information into other networks.

Don't forget that it really is a part of your job as manager to patiently tend the networks and keep them honest with different information and new interpretations when appropriate. If you don't, on the same principle that nature abhors a vacuum, your subordinates will fill the information vacuum with anything and everything. Your power as a manager rests heavily on counteracting what you can't prevent.

USING SELECTION TO REDUCE CONFLICT

Over the years, an idea has taken root that people in any particular working unit should be heterogeneous. The theory is that diversity breeds competition and keeps people working harder and more productively if they are all somewhat alike in values, background, education, life-style, and so on. To some extent it is true. People who are unlike those they work with will tend to do one of two things: They will either work harder or withdraw from the competition. In either case, they will become more involved in office politics.

As a manager, you have a great deal of control over the political atmosphere in your work unit. You can choose the kinds of people who either improve the atmosphere or stir things up through the hiring process. If you buy the diversity theory, you also buy the idea that office politics will take more of your time. Resolving conflicts will be a bigger part of your work load. Why is that so?

It is always easier for a manager to manage people with whom he or she has rapport. That rapport is most likely to develop when subordinates share basic work values, and some personal values, with the manager. For instance, if Lynn, the manager of the customer services department, is rather quiet and doesn't have an autocratic style, she will have trouble if she chooses subordinates with opposite styles and personality types. The first time Hal challenges her authority, even on something trivial, he'll do it loudly and openly, as is *his* style. He won't particularly notice the contrast in styles, but others in the department will.

No matter how Lynn responds, her response will be softer, or seem so, to those who observe the scene. She will seem to be less powerful even though her power has not been formally diminished. It has been diminished informally. The theme of this book has been that power relationships are always fluid and that behavior on the part of each participant affects the balance and distribution of that power. The more contrast there is between the manager and subordinates, the more fluid the manager's power.

If you want to increase productivity and reduce conflict, you've got to match your values to those of the people you hire. The better the fit in work styles, the less conflict. Most managers worry more about technical skills than they do about work styles. This is a mistake. If there are three candidates for a job, each with roughly comparable technical skills, the most important selection criterion should be the degree of compatibility with both manager and peers.

It is not true that skills are associated with any particular personality type. In sales, successful salespeople range from backslapping, glad-handing Dale Carnegie graduates to sensitive, aesthetic types with quiet manners and personalities. There may be times when the need to hire someone is so critical that very few candidates are available to select from. In that case, try to cut your losses. Buy the person least *unlike* the group.

Many people are offended by the concept of screening for personality type rather than just skills. If you remember chapter 1, we talked about the work equation. We said then that style is very important both to the manager and the employee. Incompatibility of styles tends to produce friction and lower productivity and to increase destructive politics.

What kinds of questions will help you get to the issues of work style and personality type? If you use the interview creatively, you'll ask some of the following:

1. *What did you like best about the manager you worked for on your last job? What did you like least?*

2. *What kinds of people did you work with on your last job? Tell me something about their personalities and work styles.*

You will want to listen very carefully for tones of approval or disapproval as the candidate answers these questions. What the prospect disapproves of may be just what you'll be asking him or her to do or vice versa. Look at the candidate's body language. What is the candidate saying about his or her peers? (Of course, you've analyzed your own subordinates so that you have some feeling for their personalities.)

3. *Describe some of the people you've most enjoyed working with.*

Look for indications of personality types.

4. *If you could have changed the work environment in your previous company in any way, what would you have done?*

Listen for physical as well as interpersonal conditions. In our research, physical characteristics seemed to bug people as much and as often as interpersonal problems. For instance, we have heard tremendous numbers of complaints about the use of shoulder-high dividers between desks, rather than private offices. The feeling that management is always watching the worker—who frequently can't be sure when this takes place—drives some employees to nonproductivity. If you have cubicles instead of offices, ask whether this is a problem for the applicant. Oddly enough, cubicles are more detested and more often rejected than an open area with many desks side by side. In an open area, everybody knows who's looking at whom and when.

5. *What most appeals to you about this job?*

If the person gives a fairly standard answer, such as "the challenge," "the chance to grow," or "the salary," pursue the matter. Ask if any or all of these things were inadequate or nonexistent in the previous job. What you are looking for is the value the person assigns to any one element of the job. If the candidate values money above all other job characteristics, how does this compare with the values of the people you already manage? Will this person, if hired, cause problems with his or her views? (Kennedy's corollary: Never hire a hard-charging, greedy type into a nonprofit. He or she will make more people unhappy than you can restore to tranquility.)

6. *How well did you like the people you worked with before? Do you still see any of them?*

Beware of the candidate who never has lunch or a drink with any of the people he or she worked with previously. It's possible in a large metropolitan area that distance is a problem. Maybe it's simply too far to go. On the other hand, human nature is such that even though someone has left the company, he or she has a curiosity about what those who remain are doing. The more negative the circumstances under which he or she left, the more painful any further contact may be. By asking the question you may get an idea of how traumatic the experience was for that person.

You'll think of other questions that can help fill out the picture of the candidate you're putting together. This process is not nearly as time-consuming as going over the material on the résumé with the candidate. Personnel has already done that anyway. It's a thousand times more revealing to talk with the candidate as we've described. You are not buying a set of skills carried around by a body. You are buying a whole person.

Any part of that person may cause you trouble, and you'll have to evaluate each part critically. As with every other political and quasi-political decision, do not go against your gut reaction. If you instinctively dislike the individual, don't hire her or him. It's so much more difficult and uncomfortable and disruptive to your people to get rid of someone who's causing problems, particularly people problems. Screen your people out on the front end.

When you're using the tools of analysis to select employees, keep in mind that if the candidate's peers are not enthusiastic, the prospect for success isn't very good. This is especially true if you expect close cooperation among your subordinates. Many managers, especially those who have a more authoritarian style, think that if a person is hired, it's up to the peers to accept him or her without question. It won't happen, and you can't make it happen. Don't buy unnecessary grief by trying to graft a rose onto a tulip stem. It can't be done without doing harm to both.

Don't allow anyone to rush you through the selection process or to present only one candidate on a take-it-or-leave-it basis. If personnel can't or won't produce more than one at a time, develop your own recruiting resources. Get help from trade and professional associations in the skills areas you need. Ask at other organizations to which you belong. Even ask the bartender at the watering spot where people of the kind you need are said to hang out! Your bartender may be the one person you tell when you're unemployed even just to win a free drink or the sympathy vote.

Keep track of the people who didn't make it in your work group. Why didn't they? If they had political problems with you or their peers, look closely at those problems. How could you have discovered that such problems would arise before you hired that person? Are there any patterns in your hiring failures? What are your biases?

Paula had a tendency to hire secretaries who were very efficient, neat, and organized and then drive them wild with her sloppy, disorganized style. She was forever losing important pieces of work. The efficient secretary would last about six months until she'd give up in disgust and go to work for someone who more closely matched her or his own style. This became a pattern, and the turnover in Paula's department skyrocketed. The secretaries did plenty of complaining to the rest of the troops before they departed. Only when Paula began to see that, in trying to find a complementary set of skills, she'd set secretaries up to fail did she back off from her theory and look for someone whose personality and work style more nearly matched her own.

Don't expect the stereotypes of certain professions to have much validity. There are thousands of data-processing people with excellent interpersonal skills, outgoing personalities, and large, colorful vocabularies. There are accountants with excellent taste in everything from pre-Scythian bronzes to three-piece suits. There are shy, insecure lawyers who shrink from Clarence Darrow, Perry Mason, and ambulances. You can match your personality with compatible subordinates just as readily as you can with a compatible boss. Don't let personnel tell you differently. It's more work for them, but that's what they get paid for. Put pressure on them to generate more and different candidates, or do it yourself.

TOOLS FOR BETTER PERFORMANCE APPRAISALS

We talked in chapter 1 about the completely unfair, tiresome, inadequate, disorganized, and mindlessly brutal process known as performance appraisal. There are things you can do, even if your company or organization has rigidly organized the process, to make appraisal much more humane and effective. It should be a tool that not only evaluates past performance but also spurs needed improvements in the future.

If performance appraisal is to do either or both of these jobs, it's got to begin with employee self-appraisal. Unless the employee gets an opportunity to appraise his or her own performance first, the discussion with the manager is going to be very one-sided. The employee will generally be more critical of his or her own performance than the manager simply because the employee is closer to all the mistakes and near misses with which he or she has been involved.

The manager should insist that each employee keep a work journal as outlined in chapter 2. It's the employee's responsibility to cite his or her own accomplishments, not the manager's. This rests on the wholly defensible theory that it's the employee's career we're talking about—not something for which the manager can, or should, be responsible.

Without the work journal, the manager will always have to rely on his or her own notes. Keep track of the problems the employee has. Let the employee keep the positive side of the ledger. It's the employee's responsibility to convince you that his or her performance has been outstanding, not your responsibility to recognize it.

Unless you put the responsibility for performance appraisal

and advancement squarely on the employee, you are taking on problems you can't afford and won't be able to solve. Employees can't expect—unless you mislead them—that you are going to sit on Mount Olympus, like Zeus, and see which of the mortals has potential. Such an expectation puts the manager in the position of selecting one employee as more promising than another on the basis of his or her impressions alone. This method produces the most vehement and frequent complaints from employees. They feel that the system offers inadequate ways of showing what they can do and what they want.

You can change that by putting the responsibility on your subordinates to show you both what they have done and what they want to do. This is going to put nonproductive employees—they had been hoping you weren't going to notice—squarely on the spot. If they can't show adequate evidence of the work they have done, it'll be something they have to justify, not a discussion in which you accuse and the subordinates defend. The hidden benefit is that, as the employees keep their work journal week in and week out, they will know early on that the day of reckoning will be unpleasant. They can either raise the level of productivity or move on. This removes a considerable burden from the manager. There is no happier circumstance than getting the nonproductive to outplace themselves.

It would be interesting if college deans began requiring work journals from faculty and staff. It would also be a fruitless effort unless colleges developed some method of getting rid of the people who have been identified as hopelessly and terminally nonproductive.

Performance appraisal is best done when both manager and subordinate work from the same set of criteria. The Performance Appraisal Grid (Fig. 4) was developed by the author with Tony Castino of Human Performance Systems of Grayslake, Illinois. It's a way to measure not only technical and business skills but also interpersonal and leadership skills. This grid's strength lies in the treatment of personality considerations as skills, not givens, that is, something that can't be changed. If interpersonal skills are treated as unchangeable, an employee can justify any performance failure as something that can't be helped—"It's just the way I am."

In using the grid, you'll need to have each employee save

PERFORMANCE APPRAISAL

Technical Skills

1. Understanding of own job (the responsibilities and duties expected)

2. Attention to detail (the standards of doing job)

3. Results oriented (the output is produced)

4. Trouble shooting (recognizing errors and correcting)

5. Other (specialities of the job)

Interpersonal Skills

1. Communication (speaking/writing for results)

2. Team building (fosters "we" thinking)

3. Tough-mindedness (flexible, durable, critical outlook)

4. Sensitivity (empathy/tact with others)

Business Skills

1. Businesslike attitudes and behaviors (personal acceptance of standards of business)

2. Knowledge of real estate business

3. Knowledge of general business

Leadership Skills

1. Problem solving and decision making (dealing with problems involving more than own job)

2. Planning (planning work schedule and priorities)

3. Organizing (arranging resources—people and things—to do the job)

4. Motivating (to act so as to achieve motive/purpose)

5. Controlling (to guide, counsel, negotiate with others)

Fig. 4

examples of his or her strengths in each area. It will be up to the employee to show how he or she has progressed or met an acceptable standard in each area. What is an acceptable standard? This the manager must define. What are businesslike attitudes and behaviors in your work unit? These may involve a dress code. Tell the employee. Don't expect him or her to look around and see what others are wearing and dress accordingly. It rarely happens.

You can't hold the employee responsible for any standard of behavior that you haven't defined specifically. Assume a zero knowledge base on the part of your employees. It's pointless to use the grid unless you do this. How can an employee tell you what he or she has done outstandingly well in one particular area when there is no measurement for "adequate"—much less "outstanding." If you can't set a measure for any item on this grid, leave it out. This means that you as a manager are going to have to abandon the old game of "Can you guess what I'm thinking?" However you got into that dreadful game, whether through inertia or because it's the way you were managed or the way things have always been done, you'll have to change your methods if you're to make performance appraisal a useful tool for everyone.

This grid assumes that, unless you are performing 100 percent in every area, you are not likely to be promoted because you are not promotable. The bottom line in performance appraisal must be that the performance on the present job is outstanding. Otherwise the manager need not talk of a promotion or a change. Unless you and the employee both understand this, there is no reason to go through the process.

It often happens that people who aren't performing anywhere close to 100 percent get promoted. That's politics and real life. In theory, someone who is in the 50 to 75 percent range (that is, someone who is doing an acceptable job in 50 to 75 percent of the areas identified on the grid) is not ready for promotion. This has to be spelled out, or employees will ignore this unpleasant bit of information.

Tie money to performance appraisal. The idea that money should not be tied to the work you do and the way it's evaluated is ridiculous. If you want higher levels of performance, reward the high producers. Don't talk about being fair; talk about who has produced and who has to be rewarded. As long as everybody gets a raise—any kind of raise—there is no incentive to improve, hence no real need for performance appraisal. If you want people to make the extra effort, those who don't doesn't make this effort know that there will not be any more money. It's simply another way of giving your troops a choice and making them responsible for the consequences of that choice.

The argument that money is manna from heaven, not a reward for past performance and an incentive for future work, is asinine. Of course, it will make the nonproducers furious if they don't get raises. So what? You haven't been able to get them moving any other way. What have you got to lose?

The stars are going to keep working—there's more money where that came from. The nonproducers aren't going to do much either way. Remember that nonproducers are harder to force out of an organization than lint from a navy suit. Don't worry about them. How much less could they do?

Try to keep your appraisals evenhanded, or at least try to have them appear evenhanded. Otherwise you are open for much justified complaining. That's another reason why it's so important to define and talk about what you expect. What you expect from employees does not have to meet any standard of fairness except your own. You can impose a dress code on your work unit even though the rest of the organization wears stuff the Salvation Army would reject. The point is that "fair" means telling people that you expect them to dress in a particular way. It has nothing to do with justifying why you expect it. Keep that in mind. The test of fairness is to spell out your standards and to apply them to like jobs across the board. Don't justify them.

Don't expect anybody to much like performance appraisals. Anybody who's worked more than a few years has been permanently scarred at least once in the process. Make sure that people know what the process involves and what they are expected to do. After that, it's up to both you and the troops to make it work.

PERSONAL FEEDBACK

One of the cheapest, most effective tools managers have for improving the work climate is personal feedback. It's also the one least used. If one characteristic seems common to a majority of supervisors and managers, it's the idea that "Everything is OK unless I complain." Instead of praise for what's done well, employees are taught to expect only negative feedback. Managers say, "Make a mistake and you'll hear about it. Otherwise you can conclude everything is running smoothly."

Somehow managers have the notion that praise isn't a motivator because people are getting paid. This is enormously shortsighted. Of course, people are getting paid for their work! They would not be there at all otherwise. The fact that people are paid to work leaves an enormous range of levels of performance. Managers, in theory, are supposed to want the best performance possible out of each employee. The harder and more productively people work, the less the manager needs to do.

Politically, feedback and praise are powerful weapons in the hands of managers who know what to do with them. They can enhance your reputation as an effective manager and make people want to work for you. You'll also have no competition, since few managers understand the process or the rewards.

Feedback allows mistakes to be corrected before they become holocausts. If you know that Laura is not doing what she is supposed to do, you'll tell her about it as soon as you are aware that there's a problem. That's feedback. Identify the problem and straighten it out. Any good manager should do that.

What's the difference in providing positive feedback, that is, praise, the minute you recognize that things are going well? There is more to be gained from doing that than in recognizing and correcting a problem. Here's why. Praise, unlike negative feedback, gets repeated. It's deliberately fed into the internal information networks by the person who's been praised. That does two things: (1) It gives the praise a longer life and more people are impressed, envious, and so on, and (2) it helps identify the manager as someone who's "good to work for." Most managers ration praise as if each phrase were worth roughly a seven-carat ruby. That's terrible political strategy. Praise is such a positive, cheap way to motivate your people! By rationing praise, you also keep your own name out of the network. It could be there enhancing your reputation and helping to build your career.

There is absolutely no sensible reason to save positive feedback, praise, strokes, or whatever you call it for special occasions. You simply can't use up your supply. It's inexhaustible. Try not to think of positive feedback as the squandering of a precious resource and begin thinking of it as a tool for building a warm, supportive, and productive work environment brick by brick and you will begin to put positive feedback into its proper perspective.

In all our research, the major area of disagreement between managers and subordinates was that of the place and value of positive feedback. Workers, especially those under thirty, craved as much feedback and as much stroking as they could get. Many looked for bosses who would provide that and had a reputation for doing so. A once-a-day stroke from the manager was not too much. Managers preferred to save up for the Big Stroke, administered at the end of a long, successful project. While the employees thought the Big Stroke was better than nothing, they wanted to divide the Big Stroke into a series of little strokes.

Employees didn't want to wait until retirement to find out that they had been valued by the organization over the years. Using praise sparingly does not raise its value. It simply identifies you as a miser. If this seems extraordinarily simple, that is because it is. Simplicity doesn't seem to appeal to the people who should be using praise as an important management tool.

One of the complaints we hear from managers is that people get "spoiled" if they're praised for their work. "Once you start giving people strokes, there's no way to stop. You've got to go right on doing it, praising them, noticing what they do, etc." That's absolutely right. As with other aspects of office politics, giving strokes is not something from which you can safely take a vacation. Just as you keep up your internal and external contacts, you need to keep stroking your people.

The aspect of positive feedback that never seems to impress managers is that positive feedback is like glue. It binds your subordinates to you and to the organization—through reorganizations, through lean times, through shaky top management. No other technique seems to do this as effectively. People want to be told they are doing well and that they are valued with insistent repetition.

Need I say that this stroking must be sincere? If you are just going through the motions, don't bother. A two-year-old can see through you. It's worse than not making the effort.

The strangest argument advanced against positive feedback is that old bugaboo, the "should" argument. "People shouldn't need feedback. They should know when they are doing a good job." How true—and how unrealistic! Of course, they should know. Most probably do. What they want to find out is whether you know!

Despite all the how-to and self-help books published for managers, the real value in positive feedback seems to have been underestimated. At least, judging from the hundreds of managers and thousands of people with whom we've talked, the sale has not been made to managers.

A manager who doesn't use positive strokes regularly and effectively can expect to get feedback about this at exit interviews. Exit interviews are the employee's final evaluation of the manager. Since the employee has nothing to lose, many speak quite frankly. One of the common themes in exit interviews is the lack of positive feedback from the manager. Whatever else the manager did or failed to do, no other theme was repeated as often.

Knowing this, it should be easy for managers to shift from a negative-feedback mode only to one of both negative and positive feedback. Nothing short of regular, sincere stroking seems to satisfy the employee over the long term. It also will do a lot to reduce tension in the work environment, a benefit to manager and worker alike.

THE MYTH OF PERPETUAL ADVANCEMENT

In chapter 1 we talked about myths that govern our working lives. The corollary of the myth that hard work equals success is that success means advancement. In theory, every employee, at whatever level, has one goal in mind—to move up the ladder to the next level as quickly as possible. The acceptance of this myth is so widespread that there are companies that will not hire people who do not, in the initial interview with a recruiter, express a strong desire to advance within the organization. "I want to be president of the company someday," the raw recruit says, and the recruiter thinks he or she has a live one.

Managers, many of whom wholeheartedly subscribe to upward mobility as the supreme value, have no reason to question it for anybody else. Their agenda must be the same as those of the people who report to them. Few studies that challenge this have been done. Indeed, it seems not to have occurred to many companies to actually investigate the number of people truly committed to upward mobility above all.

The major problem this presents politically is that, unless employees are free to reject the myth of perpetual advancement, they will continue to pay lip service to it even as they act in the opposite way. If managers want to keep productive employees who don't want to move up, they are going to have to make it comfortable for them to do a very good job in the same kind of job over a long period of time.

By putting so much emphasis on advancement, many good but less ambitious people are driven out of the organization to lower-pressure situations. It's simply too much trouble to pretend. There's also not much ego gratification in feeling like a second-class employee. It simply becomes too uncomfortable to keep mouthing the platitudes and too dangerous not to.

When we talked about managers selecting like-minded subordinates, we discussed the need to screen for values. This is one of the hardest things to screen for because most people are absolutely conditioned to say that advancement is the number one value. You get the idea that anyone who says, "Look, I just want an interesting job. I want to do well, and I don't want to keep striving," might be struck by lightning. As a manager you can, and should, change this attitude.

Unless you make it comfortable for people to say, "I am not on a fast track; I don't want to push," you set up a situation that breeds destructive office politics. There is no way in the ordinary organization that as many people as want to advance can do so, much less all the people who are more or less forced to accept advancement or be branded odd or strange. Not wanting to manage people or even a function is not one of the seven deadly sins.

Also, unless you take pressure off the people who don't want to advance, you are going to diminish their pride and work satisfaction—and you need those people! While some of the stars are politicking, it would be nice if someone were tending to business. The less ambitious person can literally be driven from an organization (except nonprofit organizations) by the continued realization that what he or she does isn't valued nearly as highly as what he or she wants. In a no-growth economy, it will be difficult to satisfy the insatiable upwardly mobile. Why pressure the reluctant to compete? There is no place for them to go anyway.

This need to be ambitious as a badge of belonging and legitimacy seems most destructive to women. A great many women, despite the women's movement, have one foot in feminism and the other on the hearth. There are a great many women who have no desire to head General Motors, though they might have the skills to do so. They are on the defensive because they feel they should want the presidency of a *Fortune* "500" company. In some organizations, if a woman quits work to stay home with her baby, every other woman in the organization is embarrassed. Somehow the new mother has diminished all those who remain. To say that being an extremely efficient programmer or secretary or teacher or social worker or supervisor is enough, indeed satisfies such ambitions as they have, is to invite both professional and political ostracism.

There are also a great many men who have no interest in advancement—and they are under equal, perhaps greater, pressure. Not being ambitious means that a man is deficient in machismo. These people dare not mention to bosses or peers that they don't want to manage people. They would be marked with the sign of Cain. Could there be a greater professional sin?

If you think this is an exaggeration, leave your office one day and ask the troops where they'd like to go within the company. If one out of ten says, "Nowhere, I'm happy where I am now," it will be a miracle. People rarely feel free enough or secure enough to say that. If someone does say that to you, give yourself a large share of praise.

Politically, this kind of pressure creates an artificial competition that doesn't raise productivity; it simply heats up the atmosphere. It's often destructive to everybody. The sincerely ambitious might spend less time looking for the Big Break if they knew competition wasn't half as tough as they had been led to believe. It might be more restful if people could stop fantasizing about advancement eight hours a day and do some work. As manager, it's really up to you to make that happen.

Excessive ambition creates instability because the tendency is to think of the present job as temporary: "I'll work here *until* I am promoted, *until* a search firm finds me, *until* I get my M.B.A. and can move on." That "until" business does not increase productivity because there is absolutely no incentive to make things happen in the present job. It's just a way station.

Does that mean you hire only people who are certified drones? Of course not. It means that you do not push ambition as a job requirement. Make it possible for your subordinates to enjoy and benefit from what they are doing right now. After all, if you don't value what they do, why should they?

PLAIN SPEAKING

There are certain phrases in the language that make subordinates froth at the mouth when they hear their superiors using them. A favorite is "What I hear you saying is. . . ." What passes for tact in most organizations begins with something both arrogant and laughable, such as that phrase. It moves along to phrases such as, "Wouldn't you enjoy retyping that forty-page report, Gladys?" or "I'm sure you won't mind. . . ." If you have been through a course in touchy-feely management and are using those kinds of phrases, you are poisoning the political environment as you try to improve it.

There is something startling about the phrase "What I hear you saying is" coming from the mouth of an allegedly intelligent adult. Any subordinate with the IQ of a retarded poodle must question either his or her own ability to communicate or the manager's ability to hear. The emphasis on "softening" language is neither politically honest nor useful. Managers as well as workers, as we pointed out in the section on personal distancing, cannot expect a love relationship with each superior, peer, or subordinate. If you need love to do your job, get into dog breeding. It's largely unavailable in business. Your subordinates know this. When you are telling them things in a roundabout way that's supposed to signal caring, they don't think you don't care deeply about them. They think you aren't organized enough to get to the point. Tact is a loser in business situations in which you must have an immediate behavior change.

If David is ten minutes late every morning, despite everything from veiled threats to hints of hits by organized crime, you are not going to turn him around by suggesting that you're sure he "really wants to arrive on time" or "perhaps he doesn't real-ize that he's holding up other workers when he comes in late." Of course, David knows he's late! He's arriving late deliberately.

Unless you are a psychiatrist, you really haven't a clue as to what's troubling the man. All you know is what's troubling you. David is regularly late. Then stick to the facts you have. Fact: David is late every morning. Fact: You, as manager of the work unit, cannot and will not tolerate this. Fact: His choice is to quit or be fired if he is late again. You will have to follow whatever procedures for firing people the organization has set, of course. There shouldn't be any doubt on David's part that his hours are numbered. If there is, you've failed to communicate.

This is really a plea on behalf of all your subordinates. They really want you to speak plainly, directly, and in simple English. As much as they resist some of your ideas and directives, they still need to understand what you've said, if only to put up a reasoned resistance!

If you have bought into assertiveness training, "I'm OK—You're OK," or any of the latest theories, buy out. It is not really a gimmick that will help you better communicate with your employees. It's thinking through what you want them to know and do and then having the courage to say what you must say. They can take it. Therein hangs our tale. Any number of managers know what they need and want to tell their subordi-nates; they simply don't want to do it for a variety of reasons.

As long as your employees control your speech patterns, you are not firmly in charge of your work unit. If there are things you dare not say because good old Dorothy might get upset and cry or Bob might shout, you are being managed by your subor-dinates, not the other way around. By the way, their not being able to speak freely to you because you sometimes "lose your temper" or "take things to heart" means that you're also not doing the job properly. Open communication means that people on both sides must be able to speak freely. If your people don't like to "disturb" you, you are likely to have some horrifying, career-crushing shocks down the road. Bad news suppressed re-produces itself like mosquitoes in a swamp.

Open communication is very simple. You say what you think the problem is and then ask, invite, and insist on either confirmation or an alternative theory from the subordinate. If your people know that you will listen to anything they have to say that has a shred of credibility, you will get more information. You will be able to dampen any fires before they've consumed your career.

If this is so simple, why do so few managers do it? The key to establishing open, honest communication is to let it be known— only if it's true, of course—that there are no taboo subjects. Then back it up by stroking everybody who ventures in to discuss something with you.

If you treat performance appraisal as a very important communication opportunity, you'll be 100 percent ahead of your peers. Many of them see it as an evil to be gotten through, not as a process that will improve the work environment.

Office politics is, in the final analysis, people talking to 1 about other people. Frequently talking is what moves power from one person to someone else. Unless you learn to use language selectively, you are going to be at a serious disadvantage when speaking with someone who thinks of words as individual tools.

Epilogue

One of the things that kept Harry and Elizabeth going at their first two or three jobs was a gallows bravado born of a perverse curiosity to see just how many ways any one boss could devise to make an employee's life really miserable. Having satisfied themselves that the supply was infinite, they began to use some of the techniques in this book.

Harry and Elizabeth's story doesn't have a happy ending. They didn't live happily ever after in their careers, even though they both mastered most of the tools for managing office politics. What they learned from their experiences was that there was no ending, happy or unhappy.

Each still had the fantasy, almost impossible to kill, that somewhere out there was a perfect, apolitical work environment, a place to throw aside the political process and simply relax and be oneself.

This fantasy is shared by a great many workers at every level. What Harry and Elizabeth learned about office politics was not to give up the fantasy but to see it for what it was, a fantasy incapable of being realized. That was the major hurdle for them as it is for most workers.

Harry and Elizabeth learned that, sadly enough, the atmosphere in any work unit can change in an instant. At any one moment things might go very well. Each worker might be maximizing his or her productivity and work satisfaction. The next day the boss could be promoted and a new person brought in. The new boss's work style, expectations, and values could be entirely different, heating up the political process.

That's what happened to Elizabeth. When her boss was transferred to the Far East division, she realized that she'd have to start a new temperature chart, update her research, reforge her internal information networks, and assess the risks. It was starting over.

That's what made Harry and Elizabeth so unhappy—the forever after quality politics imposed on their work lives.

"If only," Harry said, "you could suffer once through a horrible political problem in the office, and then you would have paid your dues."

"Yes, Harry," Elizabeth said, "it would be nice or at least nice to think about."

Having said that, Harry and Elizabeth plunged into trade and professional associations, seeking the comfort and camaraderie of like souls. Both learned that having others with similar backgrounds and experiences to share their problems diminished the pain and shortened the learning curve. Harry finally decided that nonprofits were not for him and returned to business.

Elizabeth decided that the only way to get control of the work environment was to start her own business. At least she'd have only herself to worry about. Unfortunately her business was very successful and she had to hire a secretary. . . . Office politics comes full circle.